Awakenings Press

UNCHAINING GOD

How I set God free and became more spiritual

Louis D van Niekerk

© 2009

UnChaining God

Copyright © 2009
Louis D. van Niekerk
Publishing Consultant: Crink

All rights reserved.

No part of this book may be reprinted or reproduced or utilized in any form or by any electronic, mechanical, or other means, including photocopying and recording, or in any information storage or retrieval system, without permission from the author.

ISBN: 978-0-620-44430-9

Cover by Designwave, South Africa
Publishing Project Manager - Ingrid Stegmann
Edited by Mel Lawrence
Proofread by Liz Stewardt
Printed by lulu.com

Purchase online at: www.lulu.com

Contents

Acknowledgements

When writing a book, there are a great many people to thank. People that were directly involved in the publishing of the book and people who by their presence in your life have contributed to you as person in such a way that without them, the book could not come into existence.

On the publishing of this book, I would like to thank Ingrid Stegman from Crink for her patience and co-ordinating of the project, and Melanie Lawrence for her editing work – taking my second-language English and making it readable.

On a personal front, all the therapists that have contributed to my life, but in particular Natalie Gordon, whose contribution has been monumental and who stood by me during this unchaining process. *I am eternally in debt to you.* Alan Storey needs a special mention as his insight into the Bible, his courage to live his convictions and his unshakeable love that he lives daily have made such an enormous contribution to my being. *It is still my conviction that you are a prophet unrecognized in your time or land.*

To my friends Hugo, Marius and Herbie, who are sounding boards for my development and bring such wisdom to our lengthy discussions about life that without them I could not have developed the way that I have. *Dankie vir julle volgehoue vriendskap, dit is meer kosbaar as enige geloof.*

Finally, to Melanie, my wife, who endured all the storms that raged in my head about my faith over almost a decade: my conflict with the church, the unchaining process, and all the other aspects of my emotional development. *Without you, my love, I would not have had the strength to liberate myself.*

For Melanie and Noah

The rocks of my being and the purpose of my essence

Introduction

My spiritual journey has not been an easy one thus far. It has taken courage, loneliness, alienation, turmoil and a lot of time for me to arrive at a point where I feel in harmony with God. The concept of God is an intriguing one. What or who is God? This question has perplexed humanity for as long as we have walked upright. Every civilization and society has had its own interpretation through the millennia. Much of what are accepted concepts and definitions of God today were conceived by the philosophers and theologians of yesteryear.

So, we stand on the shoulders of giants. Yet, humanity is at a unique point in its history. For the first time we are finding scientific paradigms in the form of quantum mechanics which are as mysterious as the gods we have worshipped over the millennia. For the first time when we ask, 'What is God?', we are receiving answers from the scientific fraternity that are not only in harmony with what the mysticism of the ages offers, but also help to enhance our understanding of God.

I wrote this book for those Christians out there who have dared to ask difficult questions, or who know in their inner being that there has to be something more to spirituality. This book is for those who have dared to challenge God, who have felt dissonance with the church movement, and who are feeling misunderstood and lonely in their spiritual journeys. I wrote this book because I want to offer hope to these people. There is growth in those questions, not condemnation; there is joy in the answers to those questions, not a punishing lightning bolt from heaven. I have been fortunate to walk this journey and discover that God is more than what humanity has reduced the concept to be over millennia. Most mainstream religions have made God in their image, and in doing so have bound God with chains. We limit God by what we believe him/her/it to be.

I use *God* throughout this book in capital letters, as for most of my life it was the name of a personified being. While my understanding of what God is has changed dramatically, I still find it convenient to use the term to describe the concept as it is formulated in my mind today. I also refer to God in the masculine, purely because God has represented God the Father for most of my life. It is by no means a reflection on my current theology, or my belief that God is either masculine or feminine, but rather a matter of consistency and convenience throughout the text.

My interpretation of God, as represented in each chapter, is representative of the way in which I viewed God at that stage of my life. So, while I may not believe in an intervening God any longer, I will use language that suggests he does (or did) intervene in a particular chapter, because that was my belief at that particular stage of my life.

When you read a book, be mindful of your own defenses. This is the voice in your head that tells you this is blasphemous or sinful. God never condemns or limits our thinking about God. Can the creation threaten the creator? I think not, and therefore please acknowledge these voices in your head, but don't allow them to limit your exploration. Don't judge them either; just allow them to be.

I have unchained God through many years of questioning, and I am inviting you to join me on my journey. I trust that you will recognize part of your own journey in these pages and when you do, please remember that you too can unchain God.

I offer one journey for unchaining God. Every person's journey will be unique. All I want is to give you the courage to embark on yours. My life is testimony that unchaining God is the most spiritually fulfilling thing you can do. In fact, I believe that you cannot find spiritual enlightenment with God in chains. So go ahead. Your life will never be the same.

Louis D van Niekerk

Johannesburg, South Africa

May 2009

Chapter 1 *Life as a young Christian*

To understand my journey, you have to understand the context in which I grew up, and the various forces that shaped what was later to become my own theology or, as it is academically defined, my own understanding of God. For this, we travel to my hometown, Kroonstad, in the Free State Province of South Africa.

Like most towns in this province, Kroonstad was a predominantly white Afrikaans-speaking town. By virtue of the Afrikaner heritage – in Kroonstad at least – being Afrikaans often suggested that you belonged to the Protestant[1] faith. The implications of this inherited religion were that everybody went to church on a Sunday (at least once); all cultural and official social gatherings were opened with a prayer and scriptures readings; and Monday and Friday morning school-gatherings were opened with prayer and most often with the singing of a Christian song. Above all, the Christian calendar was followed in the strictest sense.

As I later discovered – after marrying an English woman and joining a Methodist church – our particular brand of the Christian calendar had emphasis on different portions from for example the Methodists. However, the influence of the Dutch-Reformed Church, *Die Nederduitse Gereformeerde Kerk (NG Kerk)*, was felt daily on much of Afrikaner society. The problem that many Afrikaans citizens and the NG Kerk faced was that Christianity for the majority of its people was inherited by virtue of their culture, rather than their own personal religious beliefs or choices. This is not dissimilar to many other religious societies where culture and religion are interwoven, and almost impossible to separate. However, for this reason, people who made the conscious choice to follow Jesus, rather than just accept Christianity as a part of their culture, had to find a way of classifying themselves as such. For this, the notion of being 'born again' or being 'a newborn Christian' was often used. While everybody regarded him- or herself as Christian, those that were 'newborn' made sure that they introduced themselves not merely as Christian, but as a 'newborn Christian.'

At the same time, the church, or rather some members of the church, understood that not all attendees of the church were 'newborn.' For this purpose, every so often there would be a special service in which people were called to give their hearts to Jesus – the so-called altar call. This is not unlike the roadshow sermons that Billy Graham made famous throughout the Western world, and probably not dissimilar to most modern Christian communities. The point is that in Kroonstad, Christianity was part of society and culture, and until a specific decision was made, you would not be a 'newborn Christian.'

In later years, I would learn that some Christians grew into the status of being 'newborn', and could not remember the particular day or time the conversion took place. Others, however, could remember the specific time and place, and as the day that their 'old' life stopped, and their 'new' life began as a 'new person' who had accepted Jesus into their hearts and as governor of their souls.

It was on such a day in 1980 that I was 'born again.' As was traditional in the NG Kerk, for the 10 days following Ascension Day, a week of evening services was held, called *Pinkster*, which culminated in the grand climax of *Pinkster Sondag* (the second Sunday coinciding with the day the Holy Spirit descended from the Heavens). In Kroonstad, all these churches would have their own *Pinkster*, but the service on the second

Sunday would be a joint service in the *Moederkerk*[2] for all the town's congregations.

In 1980 our congregation, Kroonheuwel, had invited Dominee[3] Danie Steyn a well-known ex-gangleader turned minister, to preach during *Pinkster,* and as a result the town had asked him to preach at the joint meeting. Dominee Steyn was a very passionate preacher in the mould of most of the charismatic Christian preachers today. He knew how to 'lay the guilt on you thick', before offering the salvation for this guilt in the form of Jesus Christ.

So, on that Sunday afternoon Dominee Steyn made an altar call and invited anybody who wanted 'Christ to come into their lives', to stand up as a token of his or her decision. In my seven-year-old mind, all that Dominee Steyn had said that week made sense to me, and so at around four o'clock on 18 May 1980, I became a 'newborn Christian.' My mother accompanied me to the backroom, where Dominee Steyn met all those who had made the same decision that day: around forty people, of whom I was by far the youngest.

So what did this mean to me? Sadly, not much. I would like to say that my parents took special care to guide me through this life-changing decision, or that they helped me to understand the special implications of this decision, but this was not the case. I remember my mother buying me a daily devotional book about two years later, but in context I think my brother got one too, and he had not made any 'special decisions' that I was aware of. Yet, nobody would know this difference between my brother and me, as we both went to *kinderkrans*[4] every Wednesday afternoon and to Sunday School every Sunday. We were very loyal attendees and received gold seals for regular attendance at the end of each year.

On Wednesday afternoons after *kinderkrans* we would go to *Voortrekkers,*[5] which was an extra-curricular activity at school. The Voortrekkers had an enormous influence on my Christian mind, not so much during the regular Wednesday afternoon meetings, but at the annual provincial gathering on the heritage farm, Doornkloof, not far from Kroonstad in the Edenville district. Here I experienced many fun things, but in the evenings when we stood around a campfire and sang Christian hymns and folksongs under the stars, I would feel close to those around me. This was my first experience of fellowship and the one place where I felt close to God. When we looked up to the stars, I would sense that something bigger than me was present, and for me this was God's presence among us.

Those are very powerful emotions. I grew up in a household where emotions were not the highest-ranking currency. Logic and intellect were considered far more important, and while my mother could bawl her eyes out at the sight of lion catching prey, this did not mean that our household members were in touch with their emotions. In later years, through a great deal of therapy, I was able to understand just how disconnected my family were from their emotions.

So, those emotions experienced at Doornkloof had a profound impact on me. Here I felt a sense of belonging, something that I have not felt very often in my own family. At Doornkloof I learned to love my nation, my language, my culture and my God. When I graduated from high school, I wrote an *Ode de Doornkloof* in memory of the role that those provincial camps had on my young psyche.

It is important to understand that these events filled obvious deficiencies in my emotional make-up, as this is frequently the church's greatest attraction. Often, the church is able to give people a sense of purpose, belonging, love and meaning that is lacking in other spheres of their lives. For me, my conversion under Dominee Steyn and the subsequent emotional fulfillment at Doornkloof had to fill the void of being the middle child in a middle-class household.

I was often teased by my siblings for being the black sheep of the family, and at times reference was even made to my middle-child syndrome. Yet, I don't think my parents understood that this was exactly what was happening to me. In later therapeutic sessions, I discovered that much of my childhood behavior was attention-seeking in nature, and while my parents loved me very much, I did not always experience it as such. Fortunately, I was not aware of how unloved I felt, except for the contrast with my experiences at Doornkloof.

It is therefore no coincidence that my second big devotion to Jesus was also associated with Doornkloof. In the Grade 10 version of the annual provincial camp, I was placed in a team of peers from all over the province. During the week, we went to the activities together and attended lectures as a unit, in rotation with other teams. While I had fun with many of them, one girl in particular – Elrika Senekal – caught my eye, and we spent a lot of time in each other's company.

Back at school, life went on, but I felt very much in love with this girl. A couple of weeks after our camp, I received a letter from her and it seemed her feelings towards me were much the same. More time lapsed, with us exchanging letters every so often. At the same time, Grade 10 was the first year during school that I became the oldest child in our household. The previous year – while my brother was completing his final year of high school – was a very dark year for me, as I not only found myself slap-bang in the middle of puberty, but my brother was at the height of his high-school career and casting a big shadow over me. However, now my brother was at university and this gave me the freedom to live my own life outside the cloud of his presence, both at school and at home. While I did not understand it at the time, the sibling rivalry among the three of us was fierce, and it translated into me often living in his shadow.

During our first-quarter examinations, I did exceptionally well academically, and came closer to fulfilling my potential than in any other year. This was in contrast to the previous year when my performances were on average two symbols lower than this year. While this boosted my confidence, I performed well below my usual high marks in the one subject that I loved, accounting. In fact, accounting was my finest subject and I had performed very badly in those particular exams.

So, like so many before and after me, I had a little chat with God about my next examinations and promised to serve him, should he help me do well – particularly in accounting. Needless to say, I did exceptionally well, with my best marks being for accounting. This gave me newfound devotion to Jesus, and if I had not really thought of myself as 'newborn' up to that point, I did now. If being 'newborn' can be defined as the day from which you start acting in a more Christian manner, then my Grade 10 experience made me more 'newborn' than either of my earlier experiences in 1980 or Grade 2.

I shared this new devotion with Elrika, and coupled with our great experiences at Doornkloof, we found common ground, as she too had become 'newborn' that year. In fact, her devotion was an inspiration to me, as she had already decided that she wanted to study theology and become a minister – a decision that offered very dim career prospects for a woman at the time. We soon became an item, and she became the inspiration for me to live a better life. She would send me daily devotional cards and pray with, and for, me. And so, my life as a young Christian became more profound and devoted. My friends immediately noticed I had stopped swearing, and I gave them a hard time if they did. Of my parents, my mother in particular noticed the change in me, and in the following years before I left school, we had many profound discussions about the rest of our family and particularly about our concern for their spiritual wellbeing.

Like a good, devoted Christian, I turned to my siblings to ensure that they did not go to Hell, and it wasn't long before I confronted my sister, who gladly converted. Confronting my brother was a different story. He was at university and even before that time, he did not live the life of a Christian, based on my definition at the time. In retrospect, he lived an average high-school boy's life with some experimentation with alcohol, a few naughty movies and the odd dirty joke. Yet, from a purist's point of view, I thought he needed converting. So, on one of his trips home from university, I concealed a little note in his luggage for him to find on his return to university. In it, I asked him if he knew Jesus. To this day, we still have never spoken of it.

In Grade 11, our Voortrekker group at school became quite remarkable. This was due mostly to the inspiration of two people who had become our officers (team leaders): Jako Viviers, a young town-planner of 25, and Vanette Potgieter, the mother of one of my classmates. Together they formed a formidable team and understood exactly what 17-year-old youngsters needed. Our team grew in numbers and soon we were a close-knit family and known for being the largest team in the Free State. For my middle-child complex, this was just what the doctor ordered: love and acceptance in high supply. Jako and Vanette organized weekend mini-camps where we could replicate our experience of Doornkloof, and the result was the same. At least for me it was.

In my adult life, I started to understand object-relations, and how people could form better relationships. At the same time, I started to see patterns in behavior, particularly among Christians, many of which I recognized from my own youth. Yet, by the time I had reached Grade 12 I was a highly devoted Christian, who had found a family in my Voortrekker peers, and sadly mistook the love and acceptance that I experienced from other hurt people, such as myself, for love from Jesus. This made my devotion even stronger. By now, like with so many youngsters during puberty, my relationship with Elrika had come to an end. Yet, in the April of my Grade 12 year, another Voortrekker girl caught my attention at the annual provincial camp. Esther Theron and I soon became an item after we were placed in the same team for the August leadership trials. Our relationship lasted long into my first year at university.

In Grade 10, I performed very well academically. So much so that I received the highest colors that my school awarded at the end of that year. Being a part of a highly academic household – driven mainly by my mother's obsession with her children's careers having to start with some sort of university degree – I flourished without my brother, and repeated the feat in the subsequent two years.

My mother believed that you had to choose your career in the year leading up to the final year at high school. She believed this would allow a person ample time to apply for bursaries during his or her final year, in order to secure a good scholarship for the chosen field of study at the university of your choice. So, the discussion about my future career started early in my Grade 11 year. Given my aptitude for science and academic abilities, which resembled those of my brother, engineering was one of the earliest considerations. During that time, Sasol, a well-known petroleum company, invited a few of my classmates and me to attend an engineering week at their Secunda plant, an hour's drive from Johannesburg. This was a great honor and by invitation only. However, none of us really understood why Sasol had selected us or by what process. Nevertheless, in July that year I got onto a bus to Johannesburg en route to Secunda.

It was a great week, and all I remember was that the R50 (about US$5) charged for the trip could not have covered even the amount of Coca-Cola I drank that week, let alone the bus ticket, accommodation, restaurant meals, and all the material used during our laboratory experiments. I asked one of the organizers about the small R50 fee, and he responded that their experience had taught them that unless people paid something for an event, they didn't pitch up, and payment of the small fee was their way of ensuring that we did. Little did I know that this week was a week-long job interview. In Secunda, each of us was placed in a group, accompanied by senior engineers from the plant who, as it turned out, had the mandate to single out future employees that Sasol earmarked for bursaries or scholarships.

Therefore, it was with great surprise that in September that year, my parents received a phonecall from a Sasol representative requesting a visit with my parents at their home. On the day, it did not take long for them to explain that owing to the combination of my academic achievements and what they had seen during the engineering week, Sasol wanted to offer me a full scholarship to study engineering at a university of my choice. This was a great honor as Sasol offered the best scholarship available to any student, covering all tuition, accommodation, equipment and pocket money. Few students received these scholarships – and even fewer without having applied for it – in addition, this offer was made 15 months before my final high-school exam. For my parents this was a great financial relief, and we went out to celebrate – on the only occasion that I can remember that was not someone's birthday. Little did I know that Sasol would never see me again.

One of the most profound influences on my young life was the election of the prefects[6] or student council at my high school. Whether this is true or not, I don't know, but I was told years later by some of the teachers that I had been earmarked for head boy, or at least one of the prefects. The system at our school was that the Grade 10–12 pupils' vote was equal in strength to that of the teachers, and that the pupils elected the council democratically. The council was elected at the end of the Grade 11 year, to serve for one year until the end of our Grade 12 year, just before the final high-school examinations.

On the night of the announcement of the new prefect corps, I had a strange feeling. About two weeks earlier, roughly a week after the elections, we had attended a class by the vice-headmaster, directly after the tea interval. I did not know it at the time, but they must have discussed the outcome of the elections during their tea break as he was delayed by about 10 minutes at the beginning of our class. When he came in, he stood behind his desk and looked me straight in the eye. He stood there motionless looking at me for about 10 seconds before he continued with the class. My strange feeling, based on this incident, was confirmed when on the night, my name was not read out, to the great shock of my friends and peers. It transpired later that the outgoing Grade 12 pupils had not supported me, and I had missed the cut by one vote. That one vote changed my life. The election system was changed after this, to allow less weight to be placed on Grade 12 votes, and more on Grade 9–11 pupils. This was because often those Grade 12 pupils who had an axe to grind with certain candidates would use the elections to do so, by not supporting those candidates during the election process, knowing that they would be leaving school shortly after the elections and would not have to deal with being governed by the elected. This incident, coupled with my already shaken self-esteem, made me ask: Why don't these people like me? Why was I overlooked? Why was I treated as invisible? All of these emotions added to an already high need for recognition, which would manifest very strongly during my university life and my early career.

During my final year at school, I started a behavioral pattern that was to repeat itself at university in a much stronger fashion. I started to become a 'pleaser', and found I became accepted by people who would not have voted for me six months earlier. I know that on a conscious level I wanted to prove them wrong, all of them. So I made sure that I became very popular, and that I obtained roles that were typically reserved for prefects only. All of this protected me from the terrible pain of rejection that I felt inside, and allowed for the narcissistic ego within me to prove to myself that they were wrong by not electing me as prefect. There was, however, one more devil to face before I left school and that was my brother's shadow.

The final shadow my brother cast over me in high school came in the form of an A aggregate for his final high-school exams; four As out of six subjects. The demons stirred in me by his accomplishment drove me to work incredibly hard for my final exams. It was unusual for a pupil to depart from the school syllabus and work at his own pace and to his own schedule, but this is what I did. For five months before my final exams, I locked myself in my parent's dining room to study from two 'o clock in the afternoon until ten at night every day, except Sundays, of course. I did not understand it consciously, but subconsciously I had to beat him. This I duly did, and with that monkey off my back, I started looking forward to university.

I was to go to the same university as my brother, who was in his final year of civil engineering. I, however, was going to study industrial engineering. My brother, who was on the house committee of his residence had organized that I would be accepted into his residence, and during that December break I had already received my *Taaibos* jacket and tie, in preparation to go to Pretoria and join my brother.

Needless to say, I was very grateful to God for my final results, and so as we approached Christmas I felt very close to God. We spent the holidays at my mother's sister's farm, which had a Christian recreational centre on it, which my family would occupy during this time. It was during this time that I first started to feel unsure about studying engineering. I am not sure whether it was the highly spiritual site we were staying in, the Christmas season, or a combination of the two that had an influence over me, but on 29 December I sat down with my mother and said that I wanted to study theology.

It came as no surprise that my family was in shock. My father reacted in his usual way when shocked: he was angry and saw every potential negative aspect about this decision. My mother was permanently in tears, while my brother tried to convince me that I was throwing away the 'opportunity of a lifetime', since I had a future engineering career-path practically paved for me by Sasol. I thrived on all of this attention and subconsciously this must have vindicated my still very shaky decision. The decision practically gave me the opportunity to study in Bloemfontein, not Pretoria (200 km in the opposite direction from Kroonstad) and to start my university career on my own. Of course, when you decide that you want to study theology, this is 'a calling from God' and how can any God-fearing Christian argue with that. Had I decided to study language or art, or anything other than the already paved career in engineering, I would have had to justify all of this to my family, but they could not argue with a 'calling from God.' Please don't think that this was my reasoning at the time. I was very much convinced that God was calling me to study theology. I did not understand then, as I do now, that this 'calling' was in fact my subconscious that helped me to escape my brother's shadow, in the context where I have felt the most love in my life, and in a manner where I didn't have to justify the harshness of the decision to my family.

My parents insisted that I see the local *dominee* and my cousin, who was a professor at the theological faculty at the then University of the Orange Free State in Bloemfontein, to ascertain whether the 'calling' I was experiencing was legitimate, or just a figment of my imagination. I don't feel there is any way another individual can truly gauge another's experience as 'true' or not. According to them, it sounded pretty legitimate, and so on 2 January 1991, I enrolled for a BA in Theology at the University of the Orange Free State; the first of two degrees required to become an ordained minister.

Chapter 2 *Studying Theology*

The early days at *Kovsies*[7] were exciting, but difficult times. To begin with, I had absolutely no financial backing. During my final high-school year, my parents and I were feeling assured that Sasol would fit my university bill. Now my parents faced expenses they hadn't planned for, and, quite frankly, could not afford. In retrospect, I'm not sure how I thought I was going to survive financially, but I remember saying that if God had called me, he would provide. Well, if you say that often enough, to enough people, and your mother repeats this beautiful, childlike faith to enough people, somehow one of them will feel the 'call from God' to assist. That is the one side of it. Today I know that living in the 'now', and not worrying about the future, is a very good way of finding resonance with the vibrational universe, and of having your desires fulfilled.

My parents received envelopes filled with cash in our postbox; other individuals donated money outright towards my cause. However, it was my father who was at his best. He had shown the skill of Sherlock Holmes when investigating scholarships and trusts through which I would qualify for funding. I remember him finding the most obscure trusts that had stipulations such as the recipient needing to have lived in, or to have had some ancestral connection with, the town of Humansdorp, in order to qualify for interest-free loans. It so happened that my grandfather was the church secretary in Humansdorp many years ago. Then there was a scholarship in Oranjeville, a small town constructed exclusively for the purpose of building the nearby Vaal Dam. I don't recall why I qualified, but my father had found a way for me to qualify, and so my studies went on. I was never rich at Kovsies, but I never felt that I could not survive.

I am not sure that I was ready for the social association that comes with studying theology. I am sure that in a secular university somewhere in Europe, theology might have been regarded as simply another course, but in Bloemfontein, the capital of *Afrikanerdom,*[8] studying theology had a completely different meaning.

Allow me to explain. In any rural *dorpie,*[9] the *dominee* has a very special place in society. He is, after all, the ordained man of God, the final channel when all other channels to God have become blocked, and the guy whose prayers weigh that little bit more with God than our own. He is a society leader, a moral custodian and, in short, a demi-god. Sadly, many enjoy this position of ultimate power, albeit in a small-town context, and many abuse this power, as is evident from the many horror stories from around the world of child and women abuse by men of the cloth. My sense is that the role of a small-town reverend is not as simple anywhere else in the Protestant or Roman Catholic world.

From the moment you announced that you were studying theology at university during my time, you became a demi-god in the making, if not the real deal, particularly to the older generation. As a first-year student in a residence at Kovsies, there wasn't much place to hide this, not that I wanted to. We had to carry a board around our necks with our names, our field of study and our hometown written on it. So within the first day, the label of theology is truly and firmly attached to you. It's amazing that today, almost 20 years later, many of my residence colleagues still see that label attached to me.

The social pressure associated with studying to be a minister (theology), or *tokolok*[10] – the term used to describe us – is immense, and most of it is self-inflicted. The reason is that, as a future demi-god, you are looked upon as someone who should have a high moral standard and live an upstanding life. It was quite ironic that your residence mates appreciated you 'being one of the boys' and going with them to the pub to enjoy a beer, but as soon as you had one too many, they started pointing out how inappropriate it was. So, a lot of the peer pressure was a double edged-sword: on the one hand, you dared not live the holier-than-thou attitude for fear of being ridiculed, and on the other, you dared not do what you liked with your life, as society would have some judgment as to how you were living it.

There is another side to this pressure: what I call 'the angel syndrome.' In most of the elderly folk, but particularly older women (of, say, my parents' age group), you find this soft adoring and worshipping look in their eyes when speaking to you or of you. They would not speak in their normal tone, but in a softer more respectful tone as if all of a sudden you have become an angel. It was amazing to me how people who had known me from birth, who were my teachers, neighbors and family friends, all of a sudden would look at me and speak to me as if I were this holy being that had descended from Heaven. Few *tokolokke*[11] did not enjoy this type of attention, even if there was some enjoyment on a subconscious level.

I understand today how immensely powerful this type of attention was for me. First, suffering from a middle-child syndrome, the one thing that I lacked was being the centre of attention. Psychologically it is now accepted that the early wounds from childhood, in particular those inflicted before the age of six, are profound in shaping behavioral patterns for the rest of a person's life. I am still learning to understand what wounds have shaped my own personality and behavior, but I do know that feeling invisible is one of my personal wounds. This is such a subtle wound, yet so powerful. To be invisible in your household translates to never (or not often enough) receiving undivided and total attention from your parents, be it positive or negative attention. It also means that you blend into the system, that your being does not make the headlines in anybody's life, and that very little emotional energy is spent on your behalf. Before this sounds as if my parents were guilty of child abuse, it was nothing like that. It is a vicious cycle that keeps repeating itself at certain key junctions in your life, and even though I received a lot of positive attention, at those critical moments when I needed to feel special, I did not receive enough. This often happens to children whose parents have no particular reason to be concerned about the child, and where there is no reason to make a fuss, and the child seems to cope very well with most things he or she is faced with. On top of that, my early childhood adaptation was to become very independent. This is often misunderstood by parents, and the cause of further pain. I remember a parent of a classmate in Grade 6 coming to my parents' house just after school in a fit of rage because I had pulled his daughter's ponytail. My parents, regarding me as independent, left me to deal with this man on my own, and while I managed, the reinforced pain of invisibility is the scar that I took into my adult life.

So being a *tokolok* gave me ample social attention. Moreover, my subconscious thrived on this attention. The wounds that I carried from being overlooked as prefect at high school created a demeanor of acting in a way that would make people around me like me. Having ample time as a BA[12] student, I used to hang around the church administrative offices, ensuring that I knew who the church leaders were, both ministers and senior students. My subconscious strategy was to greet people by their name so often that they could not but get to know my name. It made me feel important and accepted when senior leaders greeted me by my first name. I did the same in many spheres of university life. In fact, I did this wherever I needed to feel accepted, but it was in the church that I found I did this most.

It is pertinent to explain that part of my path toward a different perspective on religion ran parallel with my own emotional development. I am convinced that had I remained stuck in the emotional place I was in, that my own wounds and adaptations would not have allowed me to explore religion and faith in the ways that I have. I am not suggesting that this is a prerequisite for anybody to be able to disentangle him- or herself from religion, but I do realize that if religion found its foothold in me in those places where my emotional deficiencies lay, then this might be true of other people too. This emotional development ironically started during my time at Kovsies.

By my second year at Kovsies, I was a very popular student. Not so much in my residence, because the façade that I put up was too easily penetrated by those that I lived with, but for those on campus I was a very friendly guy and I had many superficial friends and acquaintances. When it came down to it, all I really wanted was to feel safe with other people, yet I felt alone. The mask of friendliness could only penetrate so deep, and never deep enough for me to build quality relationships. Nevertheless, I did not allow the feeling of loneliness to occur too frequently, so in my mind I convinced myself I was doing well. The need for recognition made me do a number of things.

First, I completed my BA in two years rather than the regulatory three. This served to get me noticed around the inner circles of the theological faculty, and was a great way of letting other students know that I was no ordinary student – so powerful is the subconscious. Second, I involved myself in various church committees and campus activities where I aimed to achieve a leadership position; still trying to show my school wrong for not electing me as prefect – again all subconscious behavior. To this end, I was elected chairman of the governing body for the student church, nicknamed Ants,[13] in August 1992, towards the end of my second year. In my mind, a position equal to chairman of the Student Representative Council (SRC). During this time, the actual SRC was also up for election, so many of my campus 'friends' spurred me on to make myself available for election. In retrospect, the fear of re-experiencing my high school disappointment prevented me from even considering it. In fact, I was quite outspoken about the worldly ambitions of people who were not prepared to offer their talents to the church, but were chasing public recognition instead!

I felt on top of the world. Here I was at the end of my second year, the youngest-ever chairman of the church-governing body; my 'friends' all believing I had a fair shot at the SRC; about to become only the second *tokolok* in the university's history to complete my degree in two years; and on top of that, having just received special permission from the highest authority in the theological faculty to proceed to the second degree. This is something that again had only been allowed once and was quite irregular. Finally, I was being seen! Finally, people took notice of me and of my potential! On the surface, I could not have been happier because, as with so many cases, the subconscious unhappiness was being masked by all these artificial means, which I did in order to feel better about myself. At the core, I was deeply unhappy and while I could hide it from most, one man did not allow me to get away with it.

As part of our theological course and in preparation for ordainment, after the six-year study, the synod required that each *tokolok* be monitored annually by the admission[14] commission or, as we called them, the admission police. This entailed many things, but among them a psychological assessment and an annual visit to the campus psychologist. I am not sure how I skipped my first-year assessment, but in August of my second year, I received the call to see the psychologist. As it turned out, the appointment was scheduled two days after my appointment as chairman. For me, this was a necessary formality and, given the good space that my life was in, I honestly thought that I just had to go in order to satisfy the commission's requirements.

As I sat down in Bennie Anderson's office, I didn't feel the slightest bit of anxiety. I was ushered in, and as I sat down, Bennie took my file, looked at it, looked at me, and asked me whether I was a joker. One of my adaptations from school was to be the witty guy in class, who could 'chirp' anybody at any time, so I immediately answered Bennie that I did believe myself to be a funny bloke. He corrected me gently; his reference was to the joker in a pack of cards, not the jester in the king's quarters. I did not immediately understand, but already I felt uncomfortable. This guy was tugging at stuff that I did not need tugged. Bennie looked up from my file and spoke the words that would change and save my life: 'Unless something changes, you are bound to commit suicide by the age of forty.' This shocked me to the core. Something in me told me that this guy was looking right through all the masks that I had masqueraded in for three years. For the next month, I walked around campus hardly looking up. Gone was the guy who would call out to acquaintances across the main campus square just to be seen, greeted and recognized. I was shocked and did not know where to go and what to do with myself. Over the next 12 months, Bennie and I explored various aspects of my emotional past and he helped me to gain some perspective on who I was, and my true potential. I remember him once asking me whether I truly believed I was that guy who would gladly visit the needy old lady in the congregation, when all she needed was attention. In my bones, I knew that I was not cut out for that. Shortly after the engineering week, and shortly before Sasol had offered me a scholarship, my parents had encouraged me to take some aptitude tests at the University of Pretoria. These clearly indicated that I needed a balance between human and natural sciences, of which industrial engineering was a very appropriate choice. Seeing results from my activities is one of my core needs, and in the ministry, seeing results is not always possible.

I decided at the end of my second year that I was not going to proceed to the next degree, based on the special permission, but would do extra subjects and continue with the next degree a year later. By the July of my third year, I had decided that I did not want to be a minister, but since the field of psychology had meant so much to my own development, I was strongly considering becoming a Christian psychologist. This would imply still completing my second theological degree, during which time I would catch up on the psychology subjects that I required in order to continue into an honours and master's degree, which were required to practise as psychologist.

I enjoyed my terms as chairman of Ants. I learned a lot about managing people and my own deficiencies as a leader. In my Ants group, in charge of all the mission's activities, was Hilke Dresselhaus. From the start, Hilke had an air of spirituality about her. I was quickly attracted to her, not in a romantic way, but as someone who had something that I did not. Over and above this, when we prayed in private, she spoke in tongues. To me, this meant that she clearly was an elder in faith, and someone from whom I could learn a lot. She always spoke of what God told her when he spoke to her daily. This was tremendously attractive to me, but also highly intimidating, as God had never spoken to me, not even when I was called to study theology. Hilke always spoke of the intervention that was done during one of the mission outreaches to the Transkei,[15] where you get to interact in the spiritual realm and address those you need to forgive in order to heal your own life. It did not take long for her to ask me to go through this intervention with her. During the strategic planning session for the 27 mini-organizations under my management, there was a time where the individual teams were breaking away into their own groups and I had some time to spare.

The intervention is difficult to explain without going into too much detail, but in essence it is a process of role-play where you get to address anybody that you want to address, and with whom you felt there was unfinished emotional business. In my case, one component was me addressing my grandmother, who had died earlier that year, and with whom I was angry for the way in which she had treated my dad in his youth and the scars that it had left in his life. Of course, Hilke had dressed this up as me talking to my grandmother in the spiritual realm. This process went on for about 90 minutes in which I cried and spoke and we prayed. Today I understand that it was a huge cathartic experience, which went a long way towards my own emotional healing. Yet, in those days this helped solidify my own devotion to Jesus and the Christian cause, and again reinforced my experience of acceptance and love from Christ and within the Christian community. This occurred very closely with my interactions with Bennie, so at the time I was emotionally very unstable and highly susceptible to such influences. Hilke, unintentionally, had a massive hold on me. Following this process, I would often visit her to ask her why I could not hear God, to which she would reply that there were sins in my life that were blocking the communication between God and myself. I would repent and wait, and at the extreme I would spend an entire day in silent retreat, wanting to hear God speak to me. One night I went to Hilke in desperation, and she said that I should return in an hour, during which time she would intercede on my behalf and ask God what the blockage was. I don't recall what the blockage was, only that I was longing to have such clear communication with God.

I know that there was not an ill-intentioned bone in Hilke, or in any of what she had told me. I firmly believe that she believed all that she told me. What is clear to me is that she was as broken as I was, and had found a way to make herself feel special through a means provided by the Christian faith. My experience with Hilke haunted me for many months, as I knew that something about it was not right, and yet the experience was so true for her, and in my state of emotional instability, I just did not have the discernment to call her bluff. My idealization of Hilke's faith left painful scars in my own spiritual life. Why would God not speak to me as he speaks to her? Why can she speak in tongues when I can't? Why is Hilke so much closer to God than I am? The subconscious message was the same: God obviously has favorites and I was not one of them, as the evidence was stacked against me. As in my parents' house, others were more visible than I was, or more specifically, was I more invisible to God than others were?

This experience illustrates something about my journey. Somehow, I've always sensed when things didn't add up, when the church or individuals had offered Jesus or the gospels to me in a way that would just not gel with what I knew to be true. The thing that I knew to be true just wasn't always so clear, and in my dire hunger for acceptance and love, I had often left myself open to people with compelling views about God. Every time there was a nagging in me that something was not right, it was this deep discomfort that became the drive that kept me asking questions. Somehow, I knew that God was a God of love, and could not be as unfair as I had experienced through Hilke. Either Hilke was right, or I was right, but my understanding of God through Hilke was wrong. My personal theology could not allow for the former, so I had to dig deeper and ask more questions in order to understand God better.

But I was first and foremost at Kovsies to study theology. Studying theology, however, is not a trivial process. Unlike other academic degrees, when you study to become a minister, you are interweaving personal faith with science and these do not always go together. The science of theology is an interesting subject. On the one hand, the whole notion of theology is based on a fundamental principle of faith in the unseen, untouched and unverifiable. Yet science, by definition, is based on verifiable facts with strictly controlled experiments. Mixing the two allows for some very interesting results. While it was unthinkable and blasphemous to us, the foremost theologians of modern times were all agnostic. To us as young *tokolokke,* the whole notion was unthinkable. One thing that studying theology was not was merely an intensified Bible study, the latter being knowledge of the words written in the Bible. Studying theology meant getting an understanding of the historical context of the Bible; the cultures of the Bible; a history of the church; studying the original languages; getting a reading knowledge of ancient Greek and Hebrew; and understanding the various dogmas, in particular the differences between

Catholic and Protestant. In the subsequent degree, which I never did, matters such as community care, pastoral care, preaching, detailed exegesis of the text, and other in-depth subjects were covered.

The one thing, however, that no lecturer warns you about, which happens to most *tokolokke,* is the effect that this newfound knowledge has on your personal faith. And here the notion of faith probably requires a little time under the magnifying glass.

The way I see it, faith is built from a variety of sources. Initially, when you are very young, faith is practically an acceptance of what your parents and other caregivers tell you. In this way, most young people believe in Santa Claus, the tooth fairy and other similar fables. In a good Afrikaans home, such as the one I grew in, you are taught about Jesus and God and you even recite the odd prayer every night before going to bed. On alternating nights, you are read fairy-tales and stories from the children's Bible. Faith in God and Jesus therefore land in the same category as Santa at that stage. At the same time, the stories serve to cement the historical accuracy of the Bible into the child's mind. In other words, there is no space in any of the accounts – be that the Bible or the children's Bible or some teacher's account – for the Bible to be historically inaccurate. To this day, there are people who believe that the earth was made in seven physical days, purely on the premise that the Bible says so, and that the Bible is the word of God and therefore absolute.

As time progresses, the rational mind starts to investigate and it is not long before the fable of Santa and the tooth fairy are discovered for what they really are. Yet, at the same time, biblical education continues through parent education and/or church youth activities, such as *kinderkrans* and Sunday school, as I attended. In most schools during my childhood, biblical studies were also part of our formal education process. The interesting thing is that most classes in these environments, with the exception of school perhaps, are given by good-hearted Christians, and inevitably their personal theology or view of God clutters the process. Because it is such an abstract concept, each individual's understanding of who and what God is varies. Deepak Chopra, in his book *How to Know God* (2001), gives seven stages of knowing God,[16] all of which are dependent on the individual's own emotional and psychological development. In very simple terms, and to highlight one example, for an individual who is very punitive and who did not grow up in a healthy loving environment, it is almost impossible to experience and know God as anything other than punitive.

These filters of the knowledge of God are then brought into the classroom by varieties of teachers when children are educated about God. Nevertheless, certain key messages become clear, 'God is Almighty', being one. Proof of this is given through various tales from the Bible such as the crossing of the Red Sea, the fall of Jericho, and Daniel's adventures in Babylon. These tales became the pillars around which my faith was built as a very young child. These were the concrete signs of God's almighty power and omnipotence. Another message is that of 'God's love for the world', for which the primary example is the sacrifice of sending his only son to the world for the redemption of our sins. In later years, when I had a greater understanding, the letters of Paul, John and Peter, as well as other New Testament letters, had a profound impact on my understanding of Jesus and the sacrifices he made for me. All of these are very powerful messages, and all of them had a profound impact on strengthening my faith. Yet, at the same time, they seem to limit God. What most people don't realize is that inevitably anybody who teaches another about God can do so only from his or her own framework. This is naturally influenced by his or her emotional wellbeing. Unintentionally, such teachings, which are most often within the framework of some mainstream theology, bind God, or chain God to how mainstream theology interprets God. What the Pope says God is, becomes the paradigm for God; or what the bishop, minister, teacher, parent, etc, says, becomes the norm for what God is – regardless of how limited or narrow-minded this view might be. This is an inevitable consequence of allowing people to teach others about what can only be personally experienced. Teachings are good in their function to unearth some vital questions about God, as is evident in my own journey, but the sooner these become absolute truths, the sooner one risks not really getting to know God, but believing in a human-made image of God – much like the human-made images of Santa Claus or the tooth fairy.

What studying theology does is to bring science to these teachings. I can't remember whether I still believed that the earth was made in seven days at that stage in my life, but I do think I had come to some understanding by then, regarding the seven days as a metaphor. If I remember correctly, the argument in my mind was that the creation did happen in seven days, but that the days were not defined as having been 24 hours long in the Bible. This type of reasoning of course protects the Bible's authority. However, where previously the story of Jericho's walls had essentially first been received as a naïve child through the filters of another subjective Christian teacher, it was now put to scientific scrutiny. It was this scientific scrutiny that posed the first test to my faith.

In my study of theology, we studied archaeology and the associated science of dating societies through artefacts that are subjected to carbon dating and other dating methods. There were many others, but the first challenging scientific fact that ever brought me to a standstill was the dating of the destruction of the walls of Jericho. The latest archaeological findings at that stage dated the destruction of Jericho to roughly 300–400 years before the arrival of the Israelites at Jericho, after their exodus from Egypt. To my youthful faith, this was a shock. One of the things I was taught, as evidence that God is almighty, was the way in which he assisted the Israelites to conquer Jericho by marching around the city. So, if the Israelites had never destroyed those walls, what does it say about God? Moreover, if the Bible is not historically accurate about this, what else is not accurate? If this obvious inaccuracy lay in the Bible, which up until then I had held as absolute, what did it say about its claim to being the word of God?

Another major conflict and test for my faith was the assessment of Isaiah 53. If you don't know it, read it before continuing (see Notes). Most Christians, on reading the passage, point out the obvious correlation and prophesy relating to Jesus. After all, Isaiah was a prophet and here he was clearly pointing towards Jesus, some 800-odd years into the future. While there are diverse views in the theological arena about whom Isaiah is referring to, it is generally accepted that he was not referring to Jesus. In fact, archaeology and language dating had proven that nothing written by Isaiah was prophesied, nor were any of the other prophets actually foretelling the future. As a final nail in the coffin, the lecturers pointed out that the book Isaiah was not written by one man, but three men in three different time slots. Again, the questions arose: How can the word of God be so full of fallacies? Isn't the power of God and the care for his people illustrated by the ability of his prophets to prophesize, and if this is not what they did, then what does it make of God?

As time went on, I was getting deeper and deeper into the science of theology. Having completed the required subjects to earn my BA in my second year, and then deciding not to proceed to the next degree, I was essentially left with a gap year. This I filled with extra subjects, as I was starting to show promise as an academic and the lecturers had all taken note of this. Needless to say, I responded to this attention in a subconscious way. Greek and Hebrew are compulsory subjects until second year, but third year is entirely the choice of the student. So, together with two other subjects, I chose to carry on with Greek and Hebrew up to third-year level,[17] almost as a hobby. This implied the study of more classical Greek, as opposed to koine Greek in which the New Testament was written, as well as a deeper study of Hebrew and the associated Aramaic, the language of some of the books in the Old Testament. What I did not bargain on was Professor Flip Nel.

Flip Nel had a radical approach to teaching. To begin with, he point-blank told the three of us on the first day of the year that since Hebrew in the third year was not compulsory, and that since we had already proven during the two compulsory years that we could 'memorize', we had already passed Hebrew 3 before we had even begun! He went on to say that all he wanted from us was to attend because we wanted to learn something, not because it was required of us. I can honestly say that during all of the ten years I spent studying – three degrees through the faculties of social, natural and managerial sciences – nobody taught me more about the discipline of science than Flip Nel. The reality was that Flip Nel had a greater understanding of just how far the Bible actually was from historical reality than anybody that I had ever known. This was clearly not a negative for him as his subject, in particular toward the genres in the Old Testament, was electrifying and intoxicating. He understood why the story of Jonah was just a fable, and what purpose it served in its timeframe. At the same time, he had great passion for erotic realities, which lay in the original version of Song of Songs and his frustration with the euphemistic translation of this beautiful piece of art into Afrikaans because of cultural conservatism. He could rave about the poetry in the Psalms, and the eschatological beauty of Daniel, while making sure we understood the narratives in Samuel, Kings, Judges and Ruth. If I was battling to build a bridge between the religious component of theology and the scientific component, Flip Nel built a solid bridge in my mind between the two for me. I do remember, however, often wondering whether he was a Christian because of the ease with which he handled issues that threatened my personal faith. All Flip Nel was doing was raising the questions that would allow me to start 'unchaining' God. He forced me to find answers about the God I knew earlier, who was much smaller than the God of Flip Nel, and who has become my God today. Somehow, as you unchain God, the concept tends to inflate continuously.

While my faith was being questioned by the academic studies, my emotional wellbeing was being challenged by Bennie Anderson. Having decided not to study theology, I spent the last six months of my third year with the silent reality that once I was done with the second degree, I would continue with psychology towards becoming a pastoral psychologist. In those six months, it became difficult for me to live out who I was becoming with Bennie's help. It was as if my social network did not know who I was, unless I wore the masks that I was no longer prepared to wear. On 14 November, I wrote my final paper and on the morning of the 15th, I woke with one question on my mind: if God had called me to study theology (I had conveniently never said God had called me to be a minister), and I had decided not to become a minister, then why would I want to spend another six years studying to become a psychologist if I could be an industrial engineer in four years? I rushed off to Bennie and without telling him my thoughts, I asked him to do a psychometric test on me, and to tell me, based on the reading, what field of study I should follow. Bennie was shocked at the results. The first thing he said was that I could never be a minister. Without previous knowledge of Sasol and my early decision to study engineering (somehow it never came up), Bennie said I would fare well in three directions: marketing, industrial engineering and actuarial sciences. That settled it for me. I needed nothing more to decide not to continue with theology and to study engineering.

My brother and I had driven down to a friend's wedding in the Cape winelands earlier that year. I was awestruck by the beauty of the area, which I was seeing for the first time in my life. The Cape winelands are where the town, founded by Dutch colonists, named Stellenbosch is situated. It was without the slightest hesitation that I decided to study engineering at the University of Stellenbosch, and not at the University of Pretoria, as I would originally have done.

All the questions raised in my mind in the past three years of theological studies ignited a whole chain of events in my mind, the result of which is the writing of this book, with the obvious lapse of many years. In essence, this questioning led to a period in my life that I call the first desert. This desert was about to become a very severe desert, as I was about to begin a new life in Stellenbosch.

Chapter 3 *Spiritual Desert*

In January 1994, when I drove over Du Toit's Kloof Pass and saw the town of Paarl[18] before me, I thanked God for the chance to be there and start afresh, where nobody knew me or had a perception of me. I felt free. Free from any social pressures, created through wearing masks and inherited by being a *tokolok*. Free from any shadow anybody had cast before me. Just free to be me. This was a wonderful feeling and I was grateful.

Unlike when I decided to study theology, my family was thrilled with my decision to study engineering. They may not have liked that I chose Stellenbosch, which was 1 200 km from them, as opposed to Pretoria which was only 200 km, but they felt I was doing the right thing. As three years earlier, when I was faced with the challenge of how to pay for these studies, I faced this challenge once more. My academic results had warranted me a fair number of merit scholarships at Kovsies, while I had earned additional scholarships from the provincial synod to become a minister. These were all now converted into interest-bearing loans; at the same time, none would provide for a change in career.

I am not sure how I paid for that first year at Maties,[19] but somehow I did. I'm the first to admit that I was terrified of engineering. This was (Surprise, surprise!) just one of my brother's shadows, albeit a small one. Although he had had terrific high-school results, my brother struggled with engineering, and so I figured if he had struggled, then I might not be exempt from failing a few subjects too. The result of this was that I studied incredibly hard in my first year at Maties. The schedule of an engineering student was vastly different from that of a BA student. Where a BA student may attend 12–15 classes out of a possible 36 hours in an academic week, most engineering students would attend no fewer than 28 hours, and in the first year, even more than 30 hours of classes per week. This implies that an engineering student would have only one afternoon without classes, and only one or two periods off during the week. Being a tough course, the secret to success, I was told, was not to fall behind, and not to fall behind meant that you had to study each day's lessons that same day.

Being older than the normal high-school intake or student, I did not qualify for university residence, and thus had to live about five kilometres from campus in a backroom belonging to an elderly couple and their bachelor son. The result was that I was socially isolated. I knew absolutely nobody who studied at Stellenbosch, either older or younger than me. Absolutely nobody. Every day I was in class from 8 am until 5 pm, after which I would cycle home to start studying by 6 pm, only to finish at around 9 or 10 at night, and then I would climb straight into bed. Friday nights I might go to the campus to see whether I could find the *sokkie*,[20] but I was so isolated that I didn't even know where to find one, and so, not having found any social gatherings, I returned home, feeling rather sorry for myself. Saturdays were spent working on practical assignments, but on Sundays I did not study. I would explore the region on my bicycle, then relax, and in the evening I would attend the service in the student church. This was a major gathering of no fewer than two thousand students on an average night, and as many as three and a half thousand on a busy night. It was an extremely social event, and it was often said in jest that it was the 'cheapest date on campus.'

Even at church I did not make new acquaintances, let alone new friends. By the time the June exams came around, I literally knew only the names of about ten of my classmates. I may not have had friends, but I was very happy. I often said, 'I may be alone, but I am not lonely.' Inside me however, were the remnants of my theological studies. In later years, I came to understand that the questions that had arisen during my first three years of study were not uncommon. The difference in my case was that those questions were often addressed and resolved for students during the second portion of their studies. I did not have this luxury, and so while emotionally I was very content, spiritually I was very confused and lonely. I had questions and there was nobody to answer them for me; even worse, there was nobody who even understood my questions, let alone engaged in discussing possible answers with me. Where I had previously been very diligent about daily devotional reading and prayer during my time at Kovsies, I was now unable to do this. I just couldn't read the Bible any more, as I trusted little of what was written in it. When I approached the Bible and God for comfort, all that arose in me were more questions and more conflict regarding what I knew to be untrue in the texts. The hardest for me was that, based on what I knew, there was nothing to suggest that I should believe in the resurrection of Christ. I remember one evening in May that year praying a very simple prayer to God: 'Lord Jesus,' I said, 'I don't believe in your existence any more, but I somehow know that there is a God and I just want you to know this.' Consider this coming from a newborn Christian, the fundamental premise of which is an acceptance of the salvation of Jesus on the cross of Calvary and the subsequent resurrection indicating his conquering of sin. Here I was, unable to convince myself that I could still believe any of this, yet I knew that I was a Christian and could not contemplate separating myself from the faith. If ever I had an identity crisis, this was it, and in psychological terms, it was an object-relations crisis.

It was very hard. To say that many times I sat unable to read the Bible without a thousand questions coming into my mind is an understatement. Every passage evoked critical academic questions, for which I had no adequate answers. I felt at odds with my faith, and yet I did not dare share this with my mother or any of my Kovsie friends. My mother would not have understood, I felt. This was at a time before e-mail and cellular telephones, and so contact with Kovsie friends was via 'snail mail', at which none of us was very diligent. I had the occasional visit from my best friend and fellow theological student from Kovsies, Herbie, as he had fallen in love with a girl in the neighboring town of Paarl and would hitchhike down to visit her. I suppose I could have tried to explain my dilemma to Herbie, but he had always been a custodian of faith to me, and I suppose I was too ashamed at my inability to pray.

Somewhere towards the end of the first semester at Maties, I was in church one Sunday evening when it was announced that students who were interested in joining an evangelical group that used bicycles to spread the gospel should convene at the church hall after the service. Since cycling was my sport, which I had practiced quite passionately at Kovsies, this sounded like something I would enjoy. I listened to the introductory talk. All the students that were interested were to write their names on a list that was circulated. Later that week I received a phone call, requesting an interview with me for *Trap der Jeug.*[21] This is an evangelical performing arts group that tours the Western Cape on bicycles (and support vehicles) in a circular route at the end of each year, and travels from one school-leaving camp to another, sharing their love for Jesus through drama, singing and personal witness. The group consisted of 36 members, 18 of whom were men, and 18 women. At the end of each year, approximately 50% of the group left, leaving vacancies that needed to be filled before the next year's tour. The main power of the group was its influence over students in their final year of high school, who were about to enter university and begin their adult lives. In this group, these students found peers who affirmed that any fears they might have about their future were safe in the hands of Jesus.

I arrived for this interview with little understanding that there was a limited amount of space in the group, and that people were being interviewed to determine their suitability for the group – a notion that was foreign to me, as this was not the practice I was used to with any of the church groups under my management as chairman of Ants. In the interview, the chairman of the group asked me about the health of my spiritual life, and in particular, how my own daily devotional time was going. This was difficult to answer, and I responded that I was unable to pray, and unable to read the Bible, but that I sensed the presence of God when I cycled to class in full view of the mountains surrounding Stellenbosch. I told them that I knew that God loved me and that he existed, but I just could not communicate with him personally at that stage. By the end of the interview, I still did not understand the process and I left. Later that week, I received a message from the secretary of the group telling me to be in the social halls of one of the women's residences on Sunday after the evening service. When I arrived that Sunday evening, I had little idea what a profound impact this group would have on my life over the next four years. It was shortly before the mid-year break and all I understood from the proceedings was that the group had decided to convene earlier that year to prepare better, and that auditions would be held in the coming week for those that would form part of the mini-choir of the group. I duly attended the audition and was chosen as one of three tenors of the group. All of this still had very little meaning to me.

After my return from the mid-year break, life went on as usual, except now I had a weekly social date with TdJ.[22] I immediately felt at home with this group. These were people with a similar background to me, who shared my value system and who seemed to love God as much as I did. To get to know each other, a weekly appointment was scheduled between one man and one woman to share prayer time. The idea was to spend half an hour getting to know each other, discuss matters that required prayer, and then to pray together for the remaining half hour. For me, this was wonderful as it was a means to get to know people. Not that this was my motive, but it was a natural by-product. As with any social circle, the sooner you know somebody, the sooner the opportunity arises for you to be introduced to friends of friends, and your social network grows. TdJ had a preparation camp in August that year, at which time would be spent in rehearsing the drama and choir performances that formed the core of the group's act. The camp was also an instrument for members to get to know one another. One event was a 'sharing session', held around a campfire in the evening. The spiritual leader asked the group members to each share a little about themselves, and invited people to be vulnerable, while asking the rest of the group to 'tread cautiously over each other's souls.' What happened that night is the most unifying experience I have ever had in any five hours of my life. It is immensely powerful when 36 people share the pain of their past and the passions of their hearts. We came out of that session awestruck by the overwhelming feeling that God had done something special during that session, and we thanked Him for his grace over our group.

The overwhelming emotion was that of empathy and safety. Throughout my four-year membership, the annual 'campfire' evening remained the glue that kept the group together through mutual bonds of compassion. Every year, the feedback we received from spiritual leaders that organized the camp visits on our tour was that the love felt among our group was palpable. Often this was the only feedback – not that our performance was good, that our message was sound, or that we looked like a well-rounded group, which we were – but that the love between us was almost tangible. It is not by coincidence that every major religion of the world, monotheistic or not, holds love as its central theme. I am the first to admit that, to this day, I don't quite understand why in the vibrational universe that we occupy, love has such a powerful role to play. Almost as if it is the fibre of the cosmos.

I learned in later years through the Imago relationship-therapy theory that empathy is one of the most powerful emotions for making people feel safe with one another.

This whole experience illustrates the whole notion of religion. From the most primitive of times, many civilizations have attached mystic meaning to experiences that transcended their senses and/or comprehension: the movement of the stars, illness and healing, etc. As soon as an explanation is found through science, the mythical seems to wither and the scientific knowledge becomes commonplace. Our TdJ experience and my experience with Hilke have a lot in common with experiences that Christians use as proof that God does indeed exist, and that he does indeed work in mysterious ways. It is only when you gain a deeper knowledge through science that the mystery disappears and along with it the so-called intervention from God. Before it sounds as if I am worshipping science, I am not. Science is merely a tool that has proven over the ages to be a reliable source of information. I am perfectly aware that science gets it wrong, as we all know that the earth orbits the sun and not the other way around, as scientists believed before Galileo.

The experiences we had at TdJ were predictable to a large degree. When a group of people lower their emotional defenses and open up to a higher state of vulnerability, the emotion of empathy is evoked from most, and the result is naturally a higher degree of compassion and safety. How sustainable that is, is a function of how individuals deal with this newly established safety and compassion. It is therefore not a surprise that in the four years that I underwent this experience as part of TdJ, that those members with highly developed emotional defense mechanisms would feel exposed and scared the next morning. These people were clearly not used to being so vulnerable and this experience posed an enormous emotional risk. The subconscious would be very active in repairing damage to its defensive fortresses when their guard was let down, as previous life experience had proven the risks involved to be too high. I am so pleased to say that in TdJ the vulnerability and faith in each other's willingness to keep the space between us safe was always honored. I suppose this is what made TdJ such a special group of people, even if the team composition changed every year during the four years of my membership.

After our rehearsal camp, my social life changed dramatically. For obvious reasons, it pivoted around members in TdJ, but with thirty-five others there was enough space to explore and find new friendships. I now had three weekly social activities. First, the weekly gathering after church where we essentially socialized, sang a few songs, listened to some spiritual messages prepared by our spiritual leader, and then prayed together. Inevitably, we would split off into smaller groups after the official gathering and continue to socialize. Second, being part of the choir, I attended the weekly practice, which was normally on a Wednesday. Finally, there was the scheduled one-on-one prayer meeting organized by the group leaders. To me, this was highly social! But then again, for someone who had no social life, anything was more social!

From TdJ friendships developed that I hold dear to this day. Most of my closest friends come from the four years I spent in the group. Of the group of 36, sixteen of us that joined in 1994 were still members by 1997. So after four years of living so close to these people and spending so much time with them, the bonds became quite strong. Something one of the ministers told me early during my time at Stellenbosch gave me comfort. When telling him about my spiritual drought he advised me to, 'Stay within the fellowship of other Christians.' My time with TdJ friends certainly did that, and it seemed to work. Most people in TdJ could embrace the fact that I battled to have personal devotional time, but the leader of performances – who also took charge of our short sermon and the witnessing that followed – could not. To him, it was every member's responsibility to keep his or her spiritual life healthy in preparation for our upcoming tour, and the only way to do this was through daily devotion or quiet time. It was a non-negotiable in his book, and I think it was a thorn in his side that the management of the group had selected me, even though they knew I was not doing this. This came to the fore when during a witnessing session in one of our pre-tour performances, he questioned me in front of the congregation, knowing full well the answer. He then proceeded to say in his short message that he didn't believe anybody who did not have daily devotional time could be a newborn

Christian. That really hurt, and was one of only two painful experiences I ever experienced within the realm of the TdJ brethren, both at the hands of the same man. TdJ had become a family to me, and today I understand that the love, acceptance and safety I experienced in the group were more than I had ever experienced anywhere else in the world. In my adult life, I discovered that part of my own psychological weakness is the absence of proper boundaries. This manifested itself in the place that TdJ held in my heart. I understand today that it was disproportional emotionally to what it was supposed to be, but in the context of the time and my own emotional state, TdJ was more solid than family.

My first TdJ tour was wonderful and I enjoyed it immensely. If I didn't already know that I was part of a tightly knit unit, the tour confirmed it for me. I was elected vice-chairman of the group. In fact, when the outgoing spiritual leader heard that I had been nominated as chairman, he used his influence as a senior member to nominate and elect one of his close friends. In the context of the community, this hurt, as I remember the newly elected chairman saying to our management group of five that he was excited, but felt ill equipped. I, on the other hand, had the world of experience through my Kovsie management days. Nevertheless, I was happy to be a part of the group and looked forward to working towards enhancing the offering of TdJ for the next year's tour. We ended our tour, and our tightly knit family went our separate ways for the summer break. During the summer break, many of us would call one another, write, or do anything in order to stay in contact. Oh, how I would have loved to have had e-mail in those days to stay in touch, but e-mail had only just become available to us engineers at our university laboratories.

Early in my second year, my financial troubles were solved. Armscor, South Africa's governing company for the management and acquisition of military equipment, offered me a scholarship, based on my first year's performances. It wasn't a large scholarship, but it kept me from taking further loans, and together with the money I earned by working during my breaks, I survived. Soon it was time for TdJ to convene. As core management, we had to organize interviews; ensure that there was a choir leader, a drama leader, a spiritual leader, a performance leader, and a team to manage our sound; organize the rehearsal camp; and finally organize the performance schedule and tour for the year. First priority was to select leaders from members remaining from the previous year. If there was a skill shortage, say a choirmaster, someone would be recruited from outside the group. However, this happened only by exception. During the previous year's tour, the spiritual leader was also the performance leader. This often took its toll on the individual, as he had to get the group into the right state of mind before performances, and at the same time, prepare himself for the message he was about to give. He often asked me to manage the group preparations before performances, so that he could focus on his job as performance leader. It is actually ironic that he did, given his stance on my personal devotional time. As new management, we decided this role needed to be split permanently, as this conflict would always exist. We regarded the spiritual leader as the pastor and inward caretaker of the spiritual wellbeing of the group, while the performance leader was more the preacher and outward spiritual voice of the group. I was very surprised when my fellow management team members approached me to be the spiritual leader. Given the context of my devotional life and the previous year's performance leader's obvious issues around it, I was honored, but surprised, particularly as the chairman was one his best friends. Maybe there was no reason for me to have been so surprised, as I had been trusted with the group's spiritual preparations before each performance on tour by the same guy who had issues with my devotional life.

I accepted this role with great passion. As much as my own personal spiritual life was in drought, there were certain key messages that I felt most Christians 'got wrong', and I had every intention of addressing these: themes such as why bad things happen to good people; hearing the voice of God; and knowing the will of God and the role of providence were very high on my agenda. Some of the senior members of the group were skeptical about my appointment, because they felt the vice-chairman had his own management role, which should not clutter the role of the spiritual leader. Regardless of their views, my passion was to spare people pain. Already the painful experiences I had with Hilke were bearing fruit. In my first year in TdJ, I saw many people emotionally hurt because of a warped theology or understanding of God.

I remember one female member, during a one-on-one prayer session on tour, grappling with the suffering of a friend because of a violent crime having been committed against her. She could not understand how God could allow those that loved him to endure so much pain. It grieved me to see this pain because she did not understand God better. I explained to her that God does not engineer suffering, but has bound himself to human free will. It is free will that allows the choice to do evil, which is the cause of the suffering. The thing she had to remember was that God was crying with her and carrying her through the suffering, just as a father would his daughter. This brought tremendous relief to my team mate. It was this relief that I wanted to bring to the group during my term as spiritual leader. I heard too often, and saw too regularly the pain in people's spiritual minds due to a bad theology or understanding of God. Much as I had suffered at the hands of Hilke's theology. Much had changed in my own theology since my days under her influence. It remains a theme in my life to assist people's liberation from those influences that inhibit them from living life as fully as they can.

In that year, I had a visit from Herbie, my best friend from Kovsies. He gave me Charles Swindoll's book *The Grace Awakening* (1990). As I read this book, my spirituality changed. Swindoll made me understand God and grace so much better. In essence, he made me question my own understanding of God and grace, and forced me to find more suitable answers to my own experiences. One of the aspects of my Christianity I struggled with tremendously was the notion of doing good deeds. This may sound trivial, but when dissected, the tension becomes more palpable. Most Christians want to do good deeds; we are told to do good deeds – after all, I attended *kinderkrans*! In fact, most religions have the notion of doing good deeds deeply embedded in the consciousness of their followers. Good deeds are often the currency through which we believe we gain access to God; at least subconsciously I believed that. The notion of receiving something for free is often hard to integrate for emotionally damaged people – we tend to think we have to do something to deserve kindness, love, etc. In fact, Christian doctrine often states that we do good deeds in gratitude for the salvation that we received from Jesus. This is just a fancy way of saying we try to deserve it. True grace, as Charles Swindoll was teaching, was accepting grace and saying thank you – no further strings attached.

For me, the issue of doing good deeds was a crisis. I knew that my motives for doing good deeds were not always pure, yet I did them. After all, I had been a Christian for many years, and that's what good Christians do. If I didn't do good deeds, I felt guilty. It was a lose-lose scenario in which I felt trapped. Therefore, early in my time at Stellenbosch, I took a conscious decision not to do good deeds unless I felt like doing them. This was a rebellion against the tension in my head, so I almost challenged God to do something to me for not doing good deeds. What I didn't realize was that I was struggling with inner tension from a legalistic upbringing. Growing up as a Christian, the separation between what I should do, and what I want to is not that clear. Furthermore, Afrikaners like to create rules to protect themselves, rather than change their mindset and learn to deal with what they perceive as a threat. A friend who had an Afrikaans father and an English mother explained the difference as she perceived it, by means of an example: Afrikaans families living on a busy street will build a high wall to protect their children from the dangers in the road. An English family will teach their children how to use the street responsibly. While this is a gross stereotype, it does illustrate something of the legalistic nature of my upbringing and culture. In my own character formation I was now challenging the 'high wall' around me, and in doing so was deliberately not doing good deeds when the opportunities arose. *The Grace Awakening* helped me to understand this tension between legalism and the rules and dos and don'ts, as opposed to the freedom of grace. In fact, the seeds for my later liberation from religion, and stillpoint from which to challenge the status quo were sown from my understanding of grace through the eyes of Charles Swindoll. *The Grace Awakening* is a wonderful book of acceptance rather than resistance, and the correlation with Eckhart Tolle's *A New Earth* (2005) is vast. Tolle suggests that being in the 'now', and not resisting it, is all there is to being enlightened, while Swindoll suggests that living in grace and accepting the world around you for what it is, is really what grace is all about. So, while I was emerged from a spiritual desert, something new was awakening inside me. A new theology was being born, based on an understanding of grace, rather than serving a jealous God. What I did not realize was that I had grown emotionally, and so my God-image had to adjust accordingly.

This new, or non-legalistic, understanding of God was also the catalyst that liberated me from the spiritual desert in which I found myself. While sitting in church listening to the minister – who by my judgment was a lousy preacher – my mind was running wild with criticisms of her sermon, which was not in line with what I knew to be true about the Bible. I had by now become used to this, and mostly just went to church for the sake of communion with others and because the TdJ meeting was held after church. Suddenly the following question popped into my head: 'What if she's not trying to convince me that what is written in the Bible is correct, but rather is trying to use what is written and her interpretation of it – right or wrong – to teach me something?' With that, I listened afresh and the noise in my head was gone. I was able to embrace what the minister was trying to teach me, without criticizing the accuracy of her exegesis.

It was like an oasis. The following weeks, I could not get enough of the Bible and I read it with this 'new' approach. I read chapter after chapter, book by book, and enjoyed just being able to again read the Bible without conflict. My devotional life was restored! I could talk to God again, to Jesus and the Holy Spirit. I spent hours in private devotional time – almost as if I wanted to catch up on the time I had lost over the past twenty months.

During our annual TdJ tour at the end of that year, a friendship with Hermien de Wet, who shared a management position with me, became a little more than just a friendship. While we were both aware of it, we were denying it. I, for one, did not intend to allow romantic feelings toward a team mate to affect the spiritual success of our tour. In fact, I believed that the Devil[23] would use this relationship as the perfect platform to launch an attack on me as a spiritual leader. Nevertheless, shortly after the tour, Hermien and I became involved in one of the most beautiful relationships I have ever had.

We were both more mature than our peers, as we were three years older than the average member of our group. We were both deeply devoted Christians and viewed this as the basis for our relationship. However, it was this devotion that caused complications from the start. Hermien and I got together at the end of the academic year, which was followed by a two-month academic holiday during which time we hardly saw each other. I hitchhiked the 1 000 km to Bloemfontein to meet up with her and her brothers, who were there to watch South Africa play England in a one-day international cricket match. Afterwards I went home with her to Hopetown, a town that lies at the edge of the Great Karoo,[24] for a few days to meet her parents. However, I did not get to meet her eldest brother, Koos. Towards the end of the academic holiday, while speaking to Hermien, I picked up that something was wrong. She wouldn't tell me exactly what it was, but she did say that she had spoken to Koos about our relationship, and that he was not at peace with it. In context, Koos was of the 'Hilke-Dresselhaus-mould', someone who believed he held the power to hear God when other Christians could not. Koos, as Hermien's elder brother, held immense power over Hermien, so much so, that she was torn between her feelings for me and what God had 'said' through Koos.

Being the beautiful person that she was, she was willing to sacrifice a relationship with me for the sake of God's will – as communicated through Koos. The mere thought still saddens me, that one man could influence another's happiness so greatly. Back in Stellenbosch, Hermien told me that we could not continue a relationship that God did not approve of. I wasn't going to give up something so good so easily. I had endured experiences with the 'Koos figures' of the world before, and was not the least bit impressed. I believed that Hermien and I, twenty-three and twenty-two years of age respectively, were old enough to make our own decisions. Furthermore, I believed that our relationship with God was strong enough that, should he have something to say to us, he would communicate it to us directly. I told Hermien so, and I guess she came to her senses once she was removed from the daily influences of Koos and his wife, Daleen. We spent a wonderful fifteen months together, in what remains one of the most beautiful relationships I have ever had, second only to my relationship with my current wife. I met Koos and Daleen six months later while visiting Hermien at their farm. If ever I have met judgmental people, it was they. They made no secret of their disapproval, and Koos even went so far as to judge my future career. In private conversation, he proclaimed that my wanting to become a successful business executive would be my downfall and implied that I was essentially doomed. Somehow, I was resilient to such nonsense attacks, although I would be lying if I said it did not affect me.

At the end of the year Hermien and I decided that, in the next year (our third in the group), neither of us wanted any management or leadership responsibilities in TdJ and that we were simply going to enjoy contributing as a part of the group. From that perspective, TdJ was still central to my life – like a solid foundation. In the following year, life in

Stellenbosch continued. Hermien and I shared the most wonderful spiritual relationship. We prayed together, shared passages from the Bible, enjoyed and respected one another's relationship with Jesus. Hermien bought me *My Utmost for His Highest* by Oswald Chambers as a birthday gift. Chambers' daily devotionals are really testing, as they challenge the integrity of your daily walk as a Christian. If your quest is to walk the walk, then get this book, as Chambers puts his finger on the 'talk', and challenges you to 'walk.' Hermien was extremely encouraging about my own life, and her wish for me to be a better person through living closer to God was always precious to me. It is therefore no surprise that she was supportive of my next passion in and around the church: mission work.

Chapter 4 *Becoming a Missionary*

Stellenbosch *Studentekerk*[25] held the largest annual missionary conference in South Africa, and I would venture to say few others in the world rivaled it. This was a big affair during which a global missionary of stature was invited to speak for eight consecutive nights about missions, and their importance. During this week, roughly 80 global mission organizations exhibit their activities in a conference hall, which is well attended daily. The Mission Week Committee organized this whole event, and I had my eye on becoming involved with it, as I believed I had some unique skills to offer this committee.

First, it is important to understand that I had some background with mission weeks from my time at Kovsies. In my second year at Kovsies the student church there held a similar event, but on a much smaller scale. In my academic class was a guy called André Storm,[26] who was three years older than the rest of us (just as later I was older than my peers at Stellenbosch). André was very involved in mission work and knew a lot about world missions. He used a book called *Operation World*, which is essentially a prayer diary, with each day of the year outlining the demographics of a 'lost people', which by Christian definition is a nation where Christianity is not the dominant religion. André invited Herbie and me to join him at the evening services. To be honest, I can't remember the details, but I do remember that I was moved by the high percentage of people in the world who has not heard about Jesus. Being in a chosen profession, where the promotion of the religion based on the life of Jesus is pivotal, it was quite natural for me to be compelled to help change this percentage. One might say I felt called to mission work. It's weird, this thing named 'calling.' I had definitely felt called to be a *tokolok*, and now I felt called to be a missionary. The question was always: How do you know that the calling is true? Just as I turned away from engineering in favour of the ministry, again I was confronted with this 'calling.' I suppose it was easier to recognize the 'call' the second time around. But the questions that remained unanswered were where to be a missionary, and what this meant.

André had a very good plan for this. In South Africa there is an organization called SAAWE.[27] SAAWE offered a weekend breakaway, during which various missionary options were explored and as they put it, 'If you don't know where to go, go on a SAAWE camp.' I thought this was a sensible thing to do and enrolled for the May version of this camp. I guess I figured that having heard the 'call' did not necessarily imply that I would immediately know where I was being called to. So before the camp, I figured the gap year I had created (by having completed my second and third years in one) might be a good time to get some mission experience before returning for my final theological degree. In the meantime, André bought me a copy of *Operation World* as a gift, and I started to follow the prayer diary.

Arriving at the SAAWE camp, I found myself surrounded by people who, like me, were there to obtain more clarity about their 'mission calling.' The camp entailed a number of introductory meetings, outlining various regions, countries, nations, organizations, etc. I learned about the 10/40[28] window, which contains two thirds of the world's 'unsaved' people. While I was still going to learn much more about this at Stellenbosch in the near future, it raised my awareness about the dire situation that the world was in, given that Jesus was the only passage to Heaven – as Christianity puts it.

It was on the first day that we were requested to spend a lot of time in solitude, quiet and prayer, essentially allowing personal time for God to speak to us. This I duly did, and remember clearly sitting in the sun on a crisp autumn morning in May, saying to God, 'OK, God, you want me to go, so you must give me a clear sign as to where I should go. I want to hear thunder without clouds in the sky, and then I will go to Operational World, and travel to the country corresponding to the date I decided to become a missionary.' I think the date was 7 April.

Having made this pact with God, I relaxed and figured the ball was in his court. Later that day, around sunset, I was sitting outside on a bench talking to someone I met at the camp. Suddenly I saw a flash of light. I asked my companion whether she saw it and as I asked, I saw another, and she confirmed that she had seen it too. Could this be true? Did God give me my sign? I figured yes, and immediately ran to my room to look up the country in *Operation World*, corresponding to 7 April. So it was sealed; I was going to be a missionary in Ecuador. I had no idea where on the globe one would find Ecuador, what the people were like, what language they spoke or anything of that sort, but I was on my way.

Every night, during the evening meeting, there was an opportunity to share experiences. I could not wait to get up on stage to share my experience of how God had shown me where to go. After all, is this not why I went on the SAAWE camp? I went up on stage, and I shared, in detail, my experience and gratefulness for now knowing where I was heading. All my fellow attendees were in awe and praised God with me. The next day, I was due for a scheduled meeting with one of the SAAWE leaders, a missionary herself. I walked into the meeting room, and knowing that she had been at the meeting the previous night, asked where to from here. Clearly, at this stage I should have been looking for the organization that would best suit: who was operational in Ecuador; what sort of training I needed to undergo, and so forth. From the onset, this lady made it clear to me that she, and the other leaders, was not comfortable with the way in which things had played out for me the previous day. Her contention was that God did not work in that way, and she suggested that I spend even more time after our meeting in silence and prayer, seeking the voice of God.

I don't think there were three other hours in my entire life in which I have felt more turmoil, more frustration, and what felt to me like a wrestling with God. If I was perfectly honest with myself, I had asked for thunder as a sign. Thunder is audible, not visible – instead I received lightning, which is visible. It had been bothering me since the previous day that as I ran to my room, I had run past some of the camp-goers who were taking pictures with a camera flash. It created enormous doubt in me, which I simply put down to the Devil creating doubt, as I believed he did not want me to be a missionary and clearly not to go to Ecuador. Now I faced this turmoil. Did God send me a sign, or was it my own creation? If God had not sent the sign, why not? Why, if I was willing to offer my life up for him, did he not have the decency to send me a sign at least, when I had asked for one? Surely this was a fair request. And so, I wrestled with my own thoughts for over three hours. The closing meeting had already started as I continued to wrestle with these questions. Today I understand that the turmoil was the tension of going into that meeting and admitting that I was wrong, combined with a dire need to feel loved and communicated to by God. In the end, I opened my Bible on a random page, at Habakkuk 2–3, and found some comforting words. What about those words comforted me exactly, I cannot recall. Going into the meeting, other individuals had already started to share their experiences and I was terrified to do so, but eventually I got up there. I cried as I shared that I had not received a sign from God, and that I would not be going to Ecuador.

This episode illustrates a number of significant themes that repeated themselves throughout my Christian life: first, the utter need to hear the voice of God, not audibly, but to be perfectly sure that God wills me to do something; second, the enormous power of recognition that exists within the Christian community when one is seen to act in a selfless manner on God's behalf. Coupled with this was the timing. It was my second year at Kovsies – the year of Hilke, Bennie, Ants and so much turmoil. In retrospect, it was the most volatile and emotionally unstable I have ever felt in my life. I understand today that this was part of my battle for independence, the creation of my own identity, and the start of my liberation from cultural and religious confinement.

When I had set my sights on the Mission Week Committee in Stellenbosch, there was some history. By then, my character had settled and I was less subject to external forces in my life. In fact, after my 'spiritual desert', I had emerged with my own theology and was less susceptible to silly and irresponsible interactions with God. In a way, my locus of control had started to shift from external to internal, so that what I believed God to be became more valid than what my external world believed God to be. I had also discovered through a fundraising campaign that I had initiated in my first year with TdJ that I had a talent for fundraising. In fact, even at Kovsies I had always found sponsors to fund our activities. With this in mind, and given that all church activities are always in need of fundraising and/or sponsorship, I applied for the position that was in charge of sponsorship within the Mission Week Committee. It's not difficult for me now to realize that I wanted to be seen as part of the inner-circle of this mega-event, and the added justification was that this was part of a mission effort. I was duly appointed, with the responsibility of securing as much sponsorship as possible for the following year's event.

The primary sponsorship I had to find was for our speaker, who fortunately had immigrated to South Africa and now lived in Pretoria. Michael and Rosemary Hack are members of Operation Mobilization (OM),[29] and had moved to South Africa as part of an effort to mobilize more missionaries. They had spent time in the Middle East and India, and were very experienced missionaries. It was not too difficult to secure sponsorships for their flights, accommodation and transport during the mission week. In fact, any sponsorship effort for church activity is not too difficult, particularly in the Afrikaans business community. All you have to do is mention that this is an effort for God and people lose perspective of the business value of the sponsorship, or its absence, and engage more at a charitable level. I was fortunate that the newly appointed MD of Nationwide Airlines was Afrikaans, and because the airline was new, it had seats to spare on every flight. I was later asked at little notice, to find three more seats, which I did through Nationwide Airlines. The occupants of these five seats, in particular three of them, started a completely new chapter in my life.

Mike Hack has a wonderful talent for encouraging people. It was my duty during mission week to drive him to and from his quarters, and to ensure that Rose and he were looked after in general. The three additional seats were for their presentation team, which in essence was a four-man industrial theatre group, illustrating what they thought to be the harsh religious fanaticism reigning in most Muslim countries,[30] with Rose making up the fourth member. During this time, I spent a lot of time with Mike and Rose and, of course, my need to feel important played to this. I have also discovered in later years that I grew up without a proper father figure, and that I often found that people such as Mike played the father figure in my life. We very quickly formed a good relationship, as I suppose Mike had a need for a disciple such as me, and I was happy to play that role. I formed this type of bond with Mike, and to a lesser degree with Rose, and Marco Blankenburgh, who was one of the presentation team members.

After the mission week, a new committee had to be elected from the applications, and a chairman selected from existing members who were staying on. It did not take long for me to be nominated and then elected as chairman. By my own choice, I shared the chair with another nominee, purely because I thought it was the right thing to do, and that there was no need for there to be a 'loser' in a Christian environment. This was an ambitious task for a final-year engineering student to take on, but since it was still the third term of the third year and I had no TdJ responsibilities, I felt up to it.

I kept regular contact with Mike and Marco through lengthy e-mails, which had by now become commonplace. These guys had something to offer me: Mike with his experience, and Marco with a business approach to missions. I had long ago lost the appetite for evangelical missionary work, but saw the opportunity to establish business opportunities in countries of 'lost' nations. Marco shared this view, and we communicated our thoughts along those lines, often more than once a week.

Meanwhile, our group went on our TdJ tour, and I spent some time with Hermien and her family over the summer holiday. I had moved from my three-year residence, at the back of a suburban house, and was soon finding myself in my final year.

The commune[31] that I was moving to was shared with my best friend, Hugo, Leana, with whom I shared the chairmanship, and nine other students. We had such fun that year and to this day, I cherish the times we spent in that house. Hugo was elected chairman of TdJ, after some encouragement from Hermien and me, while neither of us had official responsibilities for our final year on TdJ. I had, however, eyed the spot of performance leader, even though I did not say so. Having been vice-chairman and spiritual leader in the group, and now being one of the most senior members of the group, many members automatically looked towards me for this position. Therefore, it came as no surprise to me when Hugo asked me, early in my final year, to consider the position, which I needed to do for only half a minute before accepting. At the same time, Hugo asked Hermien to be leader of the drama performance, while Hermien and I would be in the choir for the fourth year running. It was such a wonderful prospect.

Hugo was a smart chairman. He understood that, unlike other years, there was a core of twelve members in the TdJ who had shared a four-year-long journey with him. That core shared a wealth of experience, but at the same time most of these people were strong personalities, including Hermien and myself. He had such wisdom that he allowed each personality to flourish in its own department, while guiding his core management and the performance management toward a better TdJ. Of course, all living in the same house, we spent a lot of time strategizing and planning the year. And as with most groups of as many as 36 people, inevitably politics and personal agendas arose. We made it our business to try to keep abreast of problems before they got out of hand, and often took steps to ensure the group's wellbeing was not affected by individual dynamics. We took the wellbeing of the group very seriously, and I can honestly say there was little that we did for our own benefit. In fact, I think few members realize how selfless Hugo in particular was during that year.

I had taken on the responsibility of creating a good performance for *TdJ* very seriously. Between Hugo and me, we wanted to make sure that the drama and choir leaders shared our theology, so that there would be coherence in the performance. All of this went well until the end of the first quarter.

During the December break, while visiting Hermien, I had a niggling feeling that our relationship was not working, but I kept dismissing it as just a phase. After all, we were talking about getting married shortly after graduating, as we were turning 24 and 25 that year. At the end of the first quarter, I knew that I could not marry Hermien, and while I still loved her dearly, I saw no point in having a relationship with someone whom I wasn't intending to marry. I therefore broke off the relationship on the last Sunday before our midterm break. I remember asking her not to contact me, as I needed to get over her. This did not bode well for TdJ, as Hermien and I had to work closely together to ensure that the end-of-year performances would be a success. Hugo and I discussed this, and we decided that the three of us were mature enough to deal with the situation as adults, and that although it might be awkward, it need not detract from our ability to create something special. I am so pleased that some of the new members that had joined the group after Hermien and I broke up found out that we had a relationship after only the end-of-year tour, which was testament to our dedication to prevent our personal feelings from getting in the way of being evangelists.

TdJ convened with its new members not long after the mid-term break and one of the first changes I implemented was a personal one-on-one prayer session with each member some time during the course of the year. I believed that if I was going to ask any four members to join me on stage during a performance, to ask them questions around Christianity, so that they could share their perspectives with the audience, then it would only be right to have already shared aspects of our faith personally with them before the show. Our performance pivoted around these testimonies, as we called them, but they were in fact honest answers from unsuspecting members to some very tough questions asked by myself. The idea was that we needed to show our audience (in all likelihood final-year scholars who looked up to us) that we were not super-Christians. Therefore, we asked questions and allowed the raw truth of each member's personal relationships with God to shine through. This method proved very successful, as members would have no idea when their turn to come forward would be, and so had no way of rehearsing their answers. These individual prayer meetings for this purpose, with members of the group, formed part of a shift in my own Christian life. Whereas three years before when I arrived at Stellenbosch, I had found I couldn't pray, I now spent at least 11 hours a week in dedicated prayer for various things.

My personal prayer life was very strong as I had now a list of missionaries that I prayed for; I had my own diary of people to pray for daily, weekly and monthly; and I still followed the prayer roster from the latest version of *Operation World.* This took me an hour a day. As mission week chairman, I immediately made all those who had applied unsuccessfully for the committee part of a group that would pray for the mission week every week. Their meeting was the hour before our committee management meeting, and it was compulsory for my committee to attend with me. Then I had my normal TdJ one-on-one prayer meeting, my meeting as performance leader with another member, and the weekly TdJ prayer meeting. I would be lying if I said I did not enjoy this. I honestly felt on top of the world. I was making a meaningful contribution in every sphere of my life, and it meant a lot to me. To this day, I am not sure how I managed to complete my final year of engineering, as academics definitely was not my priority at the time; neither was my dissertation that was looming.

In May that year, I received a message from Mike Hack that he would be visiting Stellenbosch briefly and would like to see me. I was very pleased to see him and we spend a lot of time talking. To this day, the details of our discussion remain vague to me, but at the end of it I had made up my mind that I was going to be missionary in the Middle East. In fact, a tent-maker[32] is a closer description for what I intended doing. This is a concept that became more and more popular, and the profession of being a missionary had become impossible in certain Middle-Eastern Muslim countries. As an engineer, I would gain easy access in these countries and would set up business links, while evangelizing when opportunities presented themselves. This was a personal decision, not because I felt that God had called me to do so. At that stage, I had embraced the notion that every Christian had the responsibility to evangelize, and that it was selfish not to share the good news with those that had not heard it yet. I therefore made a career decision to dedicate my life towards contributing in this fashion, and was very rational about my decision. By then I had all the knowledge required: I knew who the prominent agencies were; which one was best suited to which country; what each mission statement was (no pun intended); how a missionary should secure financial backing in a responsible fashion, etc. On that score, I knew that missionaries need a support base of people that are willing to pray for them. It had become quite common for missionaries to build up this support for three to four years before actually embarking on the mission. With this in mind, I started a monthly prayer letter for myself. In essence, I wrote about my decision; my day-to-day activities; TdJ*;* the Mission Week, etc. Over and above this, I asked people to pray for very specific things for me, while always remembering to ask them to pray for wisdom so that I could make the right decisions. It's an amazing feeling to know that 111 people are thinking of you and praying for you, and in terms of what I know today, the power that it holds is enormous. But not for the reasons that Christians think.

My decision to go to the Middle East was very hard for my parents to accept. The notion of me going into a life-threatening situation (in some Middle-Eastern countries Christian missionaries are still hanged) was very hard for them to embrace. But as good Christian citizens, they did their best to reconcile their own feelings with what I believed to be my Christian duty. For me, the process of preparation started. This did not entail much more than choosing an organization, strengthening my support base and spiritually keeping an upstanding life. I decided to join OM, probably because Mike and Marco were members, and because I felt at home with the people in the group that I already knew. As one of the steps in preparing, I attended the GCOWE '97[33] conference in Pretoria, in July that year. GCOWE was a conference of all mission organizations and had a delegate list of 5 000. The primary objective of the conference was to strategize how to have 'evangelized' the world by 2000. After the first day, there were ten separate disciplines. Each held mini-conferences for three days, while a celebration and closing day concluded the five days. I attended the business executive conferences, and to this day have not been part of a group of fifty more powerful people. I was surrounded by owners of Swiss banks, the managing director of Ghana's gold mines, and a lot of very wealthy individuals. To bring some perspective to that statement, the tithing collection at the end of the business conference was $100 000, which was as much as the remaining 4 500 delegates had contributed jointly! GCOWE was also a great time for me to network with future OM colleagues and to get to know the whole OM crowd. One of the speakers at the conference was Landa Cope, the dean of the University of the Nations, a YWAM[34] initiative. She was a fantastic speaker and spoke concisely about her insights into the Old Testament as a template for discipling the nations. She said that one of her deepest questions was why nations were worse off after the arrival of Christianity. Most Central and southern African countries were prime examples of the demise under Christianity. Landa discovered that Moses received a template (Cope, 2005–2009) from God when leaving Egypt, and that the Israelites spent 40 years in the desert in order to organize themselves according to this template. The template has eight aspects, of which government, church, family, education, economics, communication, science and technology, and arts and entertainment were the key elements. Landa proposed that salvation theology makes the church absolute in societal structures, and that its lopsided imbalance causes the collapse witnessed in most Christian African nations. As reigning mission week chairman, I had no doubt that Landa should come and share this message in detail with 3 000 willing souls during the 1998 version of the

Stellenbosch Mission Week. Fortunately, our minister happened to attend her lecture and jointly we did not even look for any alternative.

In October that year, there was a global prayer initiative,[35] during which one nation was prayed for every day, in an attempt to unify the power of prayer toward reaching the goal of evangelizing those people. Again, in terms of universal energy and of what I know today, these are immensely powerful interventions, but not in the way that Christians believe them to be. Or, should I rather say, not always to their benefit as intended. In October I spent every lunch hour with most of my missionary committee members in church praying for the designated group of that day. As much as I understand these things more deeply today, and as much as I do not subscribe to the religion or notion of prayer any more, I recognize that these were powerful times in my life. Fortunately, I understand why.

I suppose the toughest part of my decision to be a missionary was the knowledge that I would be leaving behind everything I loved. Because Stellenbosch was the place where I felt I had found myself, and had got rid of so much of the pain that I had experienced (without knowing it) at Kovsies, leaving Stellenbosch and all my friends was hard to consider. I was at the top of my game and I had achieved everything that I wanted to achieve at university. It even looked as if I would achieve cum laude for my dissertation and complete my degree. This was the end of seven wonderful years as a full-time student, and I was very aware of the privilege that it had been. In that year the knowledge of my departure starting to creep up on me around October, and I would often find myself very emotional when contemplating my departure. I realized, however, that it did nobody any good for me to be emotional and weepy about my departure, and I soon snapped out of it, allowing myself to fully enjoy my last weeks in Stellenbosch. Stellenbosch left such a tremendous impression on me that, to this day, it is the place I treasure most.

So, I was due to report to OM's training facilities on 5 January 1998.

I went through what was probably my best TdJ tour at the end of my final year. The break-up of Hermien and me had no effect on the team, and jointly we put up quite a good performance. Spiritually I felt very powerful and do not recall another time in my life when I felt so in touch with God, without being in the 'Hilke-Dresselhaus-mould.' On the contrary, I felt that I was starting to figure God out, and, in most cases, I did not agree with what generally accepted church dogma taught about God. I made it my business to share a different dogma about God: one that was less constraining, pivoting around my conviction that God is love, and that is unchanging. If any dogma came into conflict with my own, I dismissed it. In essence, I had become completely independent in my thoughts about God, and there was little that I learned from dogma and those that delivered it. This may sound like a reckless position to hold but, in contrast, I had become completely independent in my thoughts, and my theology was very simple and very sound: God is love, and if what you do does not reflect that, you are off the mark.

The last thing I planned to do that year was what any good missionary should do: visit your support base. One of the fundamentals of being a successful missionary is to remain in touch with your support base, and keep them updated. For this purpose, I had scheduled a tour of everybody that supported me in prayer for the first week of January, just before I started my training at OM.

I left Stellenbosch with a heavy heart. I said good-bye to my closest friend and companion, Hugo, not knowing whether I would ever see him again, and headed for my parents' home some 1 200 km north. From there I would start my tour of supporters, all of whom were within 400 km of my parents' home. I planned a circular route, starting in Bloemfontein with Martin Viljoen; my ex-prayer partner from Stellenbosch, Bennie Anderson; my theology cousin Fanie; and then on to other family in Kimberley; Welkom; friends in Bothaville; back home; and finally on to Johannesburg to the last set of family. I was deeply surprised when I found that Martin was not so excited about my missionary plans. Martin was the custodian for mission work in Stellenbosch in my first two years there and in my third (his last year), while I was committee member fundraising for mission week, we shared a lot and eventually formed a prayer triplet with Nic van Schalkwyk. Of anyone, I thought Martin would be thrilled about my missionary plans. He was quite forthcoming in his discomfort, and while he could not be specific, he did say that he just didn't see me as a missionary. As I left him, I thought that he had a right to his own opinion, and that I had spent seven months praying with 111 other people who helped to ensure that I was not making an emotional or irrational decision.

Next, I drove to Bennie, and while he was complimentary about the way in which I had gone about my plans, after some settling in, he too challenged me on my decision. Bennie, who knew me on a therapeutic level, asked one simple question: whether I could see myself fitting into the strict structures of a global mission organization. He very much doubted that my freethinking spirit and evolved theology could be confined to a very traditional and law-abiding hierarchical organization. I left Bennie, and between him and Martin, the seeds of doubt were sown.

From Bennie I saw Fanie, who was the one who had helped affirm my decision to study theology seven years previously. While Fanie was not challenging and quite supportive, my mind was still with what Bennie and Martin had said. I left for a two-hour drive to my aunt and uncle's farm in Kimberley. On the way, I phoned Hugo. Nobody in the world understood me better than Hugo did, and nobody had walked the path of preparation with me, during the previous month, more closely than he had. I shared what Martin and Bennie had said with him. While I made no decisions, and came to no conclusions, I was less certain of my decision to be a missionary.

By the time I reached my aunt and uncle's home, I was very unclear as to whether I would definitely be checking in on 5 January. I did not want to create this expectation, only to have to go back and explain myself. Therefore, I positioned my visit as a courtesy one to say thank you for their emotional and prayer support, and to inform them that I might be going to Saudi Arabia, but that this decision was not final. It had pretty much been final since September and anybody that paid attention would have known that something was up, but I suppose people were not so attuned to my whereabouts as I would have liked to believe. On my way back, I visited a school friend in Bothaville, who told me that whatever I decided, God would be OK with it. Yet, I could not shake the feeling that God had intervened through Bennie and Martin, and that he was being very clear about his will for me. For a change in my life, I felt that God was speaking to me and that he was telling me not to go.

Back with my parents, I explained what had happened and that I had some thinking to do. I left for Johannesburg to visit my father's brothers, and at the same time to visit the training centre for OM in Pretoria. There wasn't anything about the centre that made me not want to be there. I just remember that my mother was rather upset because the centre only had cold showers, and I would have to shower in cold water for three months. I don't recall when, or the exact details, but in the days that followed, I decided that God had told me to stay, and while I had not understood the decision, in obedience to him I decided not to go to OM. I spent the next couple of days just relaxing with my parents, contemplating my options, and wondering what I should do next, since the option I'd been moving towards for nine months was no longer present. I couldn't explain why, but something inside me wanted to go to Johannesburg to start my career as an engineer. This was strange because I loved Stellenbosch and Cape Town so much, and it would have been logical to have gravitated back to where my social base, best friend and happy memories were. It wasn't that I felt God wanted me to go to Johannesburg. All I knew was that that was the best option, and at the same time, I had positioned my decision not to go to OM as merely a time extension – in which to prepare myself for a possible re-joining at some later stage.

Chapter 5 *Broadening my Horizons*

I remember vividly how on 2 February I started job hunting. When I say 'job hunting', I mean that in the most extreme fashion imaginable. Companies were not using e-mail widely yet, and so most applications were still received by fax. I had to phone and fax Johannesburg from the same telephone line, so soon I had a system going. I would phone companies, whether they had advertised or not, inquiring about a position. I would give them my mother's mobile number so that the line would never be engaged should I receive a call back. At the same time, I had a database of people I had phoned, those that asked for CVs and those that had no interest. Every night after 10 pm, I would set up my mother's laptop with a fax modem and send faxes to all companies requesting CVs and more information from me.

In one week, I had sent 101 faxes to companies, and soon the call backs came in. It turned out I was not such a bad candidate after all. My matric results were top-notch, and I was one of only three in my academic class to have finished my degree in the designated four years, plus with a string of distinctions and an aggregate above 70 per cent. In addition to that, I knew how to write a good CV, as my experience in writing sponsorship proposals had taught me how to present myself, and how to stand out among hundreds of applications. So on 17 February I had four interviews lined up in Johannesburg with various companies, two were with recruitment agencies and four more the next day. I would spend the night with a TdJ friend.

Leaving that morning, I had no doubt that I would return in two days with a job in hand. It was an amazing two days. When the recruiters met me and heard that I was in town for only two days, they lined up four more interviews. At the same time, another interview in Paarl (Cape Town) came through from my original applications. My head still spins when I recall the mystery of those two days. After the first day, I had a job offer from a Japanese electronics company for a position as a warehouse and distribution manager. The recruiters felt I could do better. By lunchtime the next day I had had twelve interviews, with a solid offer in my pocket, and the prospect of another in Paarl. Two more companies were contemplating offers, all of which left me rather contented. I was in the northern suburbs of Johannesburg, tired and exhausted. I just wanted to go back home, but decided that since the last interview was two hours way and on my way to central Jo'burg, that I would try arrange for the interviewers to see me earlier, or else I would go past them on my way home. They did see me early.

In the early part of 1998 a movie by the name of *Sliding Doors* (Howitt, 1998) was released. In the movie a women falls ill and decides to go home. As she rushes to the underground station, she sees the train about to depart and darts frantically for the door. As she gets to the door, it starts to close and at that moment, the movie splits in two. In the one half, she gets into the train, goes home only to find her husband with his mistress, she leaves him, meets another successful man, and has a successful career. In the other, she misses the train, gets home feeling sick, suspects her boyfriend of an affair, doesn't confront it, and goes on to live a pathetic life of insecurity and feeling sorry for herself. This is what you call a defining moment. One moment in time, which had either scenario played itself out, life would have turned out very differently. My decision to go to that meeting, even though I did not feel like it, was a defining moment in my life. Every aspect of my life today was defined by that moment. I am not sure if many people can trace back their 'sliding-door moments' so clearly, but if ever there was one, that was a sliding-door moment for me.

When I arrived, the woman who was supposed to see me was occupied, and so I was passed onto another consultant, Lisa. After waiting for fifteen minutes, I was shown in. After the usual introductions and a further five minutes, she exclaimed that she had just the job for me. She had an acquaintance who had built up a very successful consulting firm in eight years and who was looking for a young engineer, preferably with two years' experience. She was going to call him to see whether he would see me, as she believed I was just what he needed. As she left the room, I knew this was the position for me. I subscribe to the notion of vibrational alignment and time as a concept, but in those days, I just had a good old gut feeling. I knew that this was the job for me. She told me the man could see me only at five-thirty that afternoon, and asked if I would please wait to see him. I gladly obliged and decided that I would go and see a movie. In the meantime, another recruiter phoned with a brilliant prospect with Unilever, so off I went to Benoni for another interview. At five-fifteen I was in Woodmead, waiting for my interview with Malcolm Perrie, MD of The Marketing Shop.

Malcolm was a thirty-nine year old engineer with an MBA turned market research consultant. He essentially needed a sidekick as his management responsibilities denied him the time to focus on the consulting aspect of the business, which was the heart of the revenue stream. Being an engineer, he sought another engineering mind, and he was particularly attracted to my industrial engineering degree, which covered some business subjects. This indicated to him that I wouldn't be too raw into the consulting world. I understand today that I must have looked like a real Dutchman,[36] fresh from the *plaas*[37] to this Jo'burg-raised Englishman. Malcolm soon asked whether I would meet his partner, Nick, who was up from Cape Town. Nick didn't really know what to make of this unexpected interview, and Malcolm was speaking to Jenny, his HR manager to see whether she could see me the next morning. After seeing Nick, he asked whether it was possible to see Jenny. I explained that I was supposed to go back to my parents' house, and that I did not have a place to stay or a change of clothing, but that I would make a plan. Malcolm put me up in a B&B, and I had to live with wearing the same shirt and underwear the next day. He also asked about my salary expectations, and by now the recruiters had coached me on not underselling myself. With the confidence of one offer secured, I shot high.

That night I could not sleep. My head was spinning. I tried everything in my power to sleep, but I found the events of the past two days totally overwhelming. The prospect of my meeting the next day was the last straw in my sleepless night. I think I slept two hours, but I got up early to meet Jenny at 8:00 am. The meeting seemed to be just a formality, as Malcolm stuck his head in to tell me to come say good-bye to him after my meeting with Jenny. As I walked in, he offered me the job. His salary offer was just below my high aim, but with a promise of an adjustment based on performance after six months. I left Jo'burg on cloud nine. While I did not accept immediately, as the recruiters taught me that one should always consider all job options, I pretty much knew that this was what I wanted. The interview in Paarl still loomed and just to keep an open mind, I decided to go and see what it had to offer. So, after six weeks of not knowing when I would see Stellenbosch again, I was back in my old house, spending time with Hugo and essentially catching my breath after a whirlwind three weeks. The job in Paarl was dull and I think they could see that it wasn't what I wanted. I had hardly left and they phoned to say I had not got it. I couldn't have been more pleased. I was heading for Jo'burg. On the first day of March 1998, I was starting a new career as an engineer and side-kick to the managing director of a big firm. In my 'sliding-door experience', I could not have dreamed how defining that start in my life would be.

Bright-eyed and bushy-tailed, I arrived at The Marketing Shop on 1 March, and within an hour my expectations of the job were fulfilled. By the end of that day, I had attended a national after-sales conference by Ford South Africa, and by that afternoon a presentation of all the managing directors of the South African truck manufacturing market, as part of a Naamsa[38] meeting. Such was Malcolm's promise to me. He would take me everywhere he went, and I was to learn the industry, at a fast pace, from the national expert on automotive parts and trucks. Those first six months were thrilling. By day, Malcolm and I would go from meeting to meeting and by night, I would sit writing proposals and reports, and doing analysis. My average day started at five in the morning, and finished at eleven at night, with laptop in bed. It wasn't uncommon for Malcolm to call me late at night to discuss a report or analysis, or for us to work late at the office every night.

I lived in Alberton, which is 40 km from Woodmead, where our offices where. So, to beat the traffic, I would leave at six in the morning, to be at the offices by six-forty. As a diligent Christian, this was a good opportunity for me to have prayer-time, and so I would close my door to attend to my prayer time until 7:30 am when the other employees started to arrive. But the power of my prayer time in Stellenbosch had gone. I still prayed for all the missionaries, countries, organizations and people that I used to, but something was missing. I put it down to a bad patch in my relationship with God. At the same time, I was angry with God. Very angry. I felt that God had played with the emotions of the 111 people in my prayer support group. While I understood why I was not with OM, I felt that they might not, and that it was unfair that they were so dedicated to supporting me, only to have me not go to where their prayers were leading me. I felt God was wrong for telling me not to go only three days before I had to start my training. It just wasn't fair on everybody involved. In an attempt to explain myself, I wrote one last mission-support newsletter, as I used to at Stellenbosch, and sent it to everybody in my support network. Still, it did not feel right.

In addition, I was angry with God because I had to stay. Why did I have to stay? If anybody was ready and willing, it was I. For goodness sake, we had organized the mission week to raise awareness and recruit missionaries because few Christians really wanted to take responsibility for the lost nations. There I was, willing, able and ready, and God told me to stay. I was angry. Very angry.

After three months, I moved from Alberton to Randburg, which was 30 minutes shorter on my travel schedule. I settled and started to look for a spiritual home. The two single people I shared a flat with attended the local NG Kerk[39] and occasionally went to the local AGS Kerk,[40] the latter being a little bit more charismatic than the NG Kerk. I attended a gathering for young working people, and got to know new people. By default, I would visit some, whom I called friends, but it wasn't even a shade of what I had in my *TdJ* social network. In addition, the preachers in the NG Kerk irritated the life out of me. I thought that their theology was backward, and that they did not understand God. Most preaching was condemning, filled with hellfire and brimstone and if it wasn't that, then it was aimed at creating feelings of guilt. Stellenbosch had made my theology very liberal, and this type of conservatism did not gel with me. In essence, I did not enjoy going to church. Yet, as a dedicated supporter of mission work, I lit the fire for them to organize a mission week. I psyched them up with all my knowledge, and played on their emotions about all the souls that were dying without ever hearing about God. Soon a group of young working adults were mobilized into mission support and organizing an awareness week. But to me it felt hollow. None of the power of my life in Stellenbosch was present, and I put it down to my anger with God. I had been in a spiritual desert before, and I knew that this was just another variation of that theme. The old advice of staying in the community remained top of mind.

This was a time of change. I loved my job and I had no issue with working 16 hours a day. I made it very clear to Malcolm that this could never be sustainable, but while I didn't have a wife and kids (or girlfriend, for that matter) I was happy to put in the hours. The learning made it all worthwhile. Not many people can say that they did a presentation to a public company board six months after university. This was the exposure Malcolm afforded me, and I rose to the occasion. On the other hand, my theology was evolving even more. Probably the biggest shift was my inability to believe in Hell, demons or the Devil. This was not a new theme. While studying theology, I discovered this interesting little fact: research had shown that most of the books of the Old Testament were written post exile.[41] [42] There is no reference to the concept of angels in any books written before the exile. In Babylon, however, the notion of angels (good or bad) existed much earlier than the arrival of the Israelites on their exile. In literature after the exile, the concept of angels and fallen angels was introduced. Much later, the concept of an eternal place of punishment in the form of the Hell was introduced into ancient Jewish literature. This bugged me. Surely if angels and demons existed, it would have been evident for all time, including current times. Angelic appearances are confined to ancient times and the Bible does not really give a reason that these appearances dried up so that modern man can verify their existence. My doubt in angels brought me to the place where I dismissed their existence as early as my first year at Stellenbosch. The problem was that common Christian knowledge has it that demons are fallen angels, the chief of all being the Devil. Now this is a problem. If you don't believe in angels, you should not believe in demons or the Devil. If you don't believe in the Devil, then believing in Hell doesn't make a lot of sense. If you don't believe in Hell, then what are you supposed to be saved from? These were some of the thoughts during my spiritual desert at Stellenbosch and, to be honest, after emerging from it, I did not have the energy to continue to battle with those questions, and so I swept them under the carpet. Mike Hack had had such real experiences with demons in Egypt and elsewhere in the Middle East that it removed all doubt from my mind. In fact, I was glad that I had been shown the light once more, and during those lengthy prayer sessions in my final year, much time was spent rebuking Satan and his demon cohorts.

Spending so much time away from the church, compared with the previous year, I could not help but think about the notion of demons once more. It just didn't make sense. In addition, my own theology was shifting rapidly away from the savior theology toward the loving theology. That is, I was less and less convinced that Jesus came to earth to save us, but more and more convinced that he came to earth to love us. What sealed it was my next visit to Stellenbosch.

Landa Cope, whom I had heard speak at GCOWE the previous year, was coming to Stellenbosch Mission Week and I was not going to miss this for the world. I was also invited to be a guest speaker at a Christian business breakfast the week before mission week. I was fortunate that there was research to be done for The Marketing Shop during that time, and so Malcolm and I struck a deal that I would pay for one flight and he for another. That week in Stellenbosch is the single biggest influence on my spiritual life to date. I don't think so much because of the sustainability of the message, but because it acted as a catalyst for major shifts in my theology and placed me on a collision course with the church in general, if I wasn't already on one. The key difference between Landa Cope's message and the mainstream church was the emphasis on the gospel. Mainstream Christianity has salvation as the goal and key offering for Christians. This leaves little space for further objectives larger than the first, which often leads to converted Christians without any further spiritual growth. As was the case with so many Afrikaners that called themselves Christians, but whose conversion meant nothing in their lives other than the burden of guilt. She calls this the gospel of salvation. Opposed this is the gospel of the kingdom. The gospel of the kingdom suggests that in each of the eight disciplines there is sanctification in vocation, irrespective of church involvement. The gospel of salvation wants to sanctify everything by making the church absolute, while the gospel of the kingdom proposes that it does not need the church for sanctification. As a prime example, the first heart transplant was evaluated. The gospel of salvation would want Professor Chris Barnard to give recognition to the church or God, or at the very least donate some of the financial gain in order for this to be holy. In the gospel of the kingdom, this deed is considered holy in itself, as it brings a higher state of wellness to all, irrespective of recognition or even whether Prof Barnard was a Christian himself. Another example is the Hubble space telescope. The mainstream church often complained about the billions of dollars being used to send a telescope into space, when that money could be used to feed the poor. The gospel of the kingdom suggests that advances in science and technology bring glory to God, irrespective, and in this case allow us to witness creation! Landa explained that a dichotomy between what was holy and not holy – as opposites – had entered the church roughly 150 years ago. Before this, Christians (Protestants) understood that any vocation could be holy in its own right, but since then, there has been this everlasting pull between what is holy and what is not. Of course, the church flourishes on this dichotomy as it gives it power. The church holds the ultimate currency. Nothing that has not been sanctified by the church, in whichever way, can be holy, which is very far from the gospel of the kingdom. It is ironic that there are elements in this position of power that correlate with the position of power that the Roman Catholic church held in the Dark Ages, and which spurred on the Reformation and Renaissance.

This stuff resonated with me. It summed up in words the direction of my own theology and in particular its development over the past four years. Landa ended the week with a three-hour session (nobody moved) in which she guided 3 000 students through each of the eight disciplines, helping everyone to identify the discipline in which he or she believed they were endowed with talents. She encouraged all to find their vocation within each discipline and to live the gospel of the kingdom, rather than the gospel of salvation. This brought peace of mind to me for the first time since I had decided not to join OM. For the first time I understood why God had wanted me to stay. My vocation was clearly in business. It freed me to feel sanctification in the work that I was enjoying thoroughly, and not to sanctify it with the 20% tithing I was giving to the church every month. Shortly after that week, it was time for my first review with Malcolm. Together with the raise he gave me, and by lowering my tithing to the normal 10%, I bought myself a brand new VW Polo 1.8 Classic – what a joy, my first new car! In the gospel of salvation, I should have donated the money to mission work so that more souls could be saved.

Landa Cope helped me to discover that the God that I was serving was much smaller than the God she was serving. In essence, she stretched the boundaries of the box into which I had placed God. Her theology helped me to question my own sufficiently to unchain God a little further and again he inflated as the bounds I placed on him were released. In later years, the notion of man creating God in his own image helped me to understand that I had found a new image of God and that the God that I had served until August 1998 was now obsolete. God did not care about salvation as much as what happened after that. God wanted a better life for all, for the kingdom of God to come to earth. That is why he gave us the Old Testament template, which Landa had highlighted so eloquently. It is interesting to note that Landa says that Jewish people, to this day, live by this template (knowingly or unknowingly) and that their prosperity is testament that this template is the way the creator intended it to be. While this was not a spiritual desert, on the contrary, I discovered that I had to find a new way to relate to God. It was like a re-birth. I knew that God had not changed, but that my knowledge of who God was, was completely new – as if I had started a relationship with him for the first time.

Of course, by now I was fast becoming a foreigner in a mainstream church. Other than from Landa Cope, I have never heard the gospel of the kingdom preached in any other church. Before it sounds as if I am dismissing the mainstream church, based on one individual's interpretation of the Old Testament, and formulating the gospel of the kingdom, let me quantify. Before I heard Landa Cope, I had long felt uncomfortable with the over-emphasis on salvation. Too many churches saw that as the final frontier, and while not too many would admit to it or even knew it, in their day-to-day theology it was clear in their minds that the church was pivotal to society's hope for grace and, by implication, salvation. Landa had given me an alternative that resonated with my own theology. I was miles away from the immature and inconsistent personal faith that I had held during my time at Kovsies. Psychologists will tell you that as an adult the personality settles, and only if it settles well, will the locus of control shift from external to internal. In my case this is exactly what happened, but I think this process was accelerated in me, because the external forces exerting some control over me were inconsistent and at the best of times harmful influences. I had the grace of always having an underlying logic and gut feel telling me there had to be better answers. Also, I continued to ask the tough questions and did not shy away from the possibility of inconvenient answers.

Chapter 6 *Marrying Melanie*

To write about my own spiritual journey without writing about my wife would be to build a house without a foundation. If I look at my life before and after I met Melanie, there are distinct things that I know were master-crafted by her gifted senses and the influence she has had on my life thus far.

Melanie worked for Malcolm's family as an au pair. She had studied for two years to become a chiropractor, but realized that it wasn't for her. In order to figure out what to do with her life, she decided to work for a year, and since she loves children so much, the position was ideal. In a beautiful piece of synchronicity, Melanie and I were formalized into Malcolm's employment in March 1998.

Malcolm had an office suite with a central entrance to his secretary's office. On the left, a door led into his office and a door on the right into another office. Since I was his side-kick, I occupied the office to the right for the first couple of months of employment at The Marketing Shop. I had occasionally seen this woman visiting Malcolm with his children, and had assumed that this was his wife. Not one to be left out (or missing out on an opportunity to tighten relationships with my boss) I introduced myself after the second or third meeting. I heard later that the lady was the family au pair, and after she had been on a ladies night with all the drinking girls in the office, I categorized her as 'one of the girls.' Because of my conservative Christian make-up, she could never have qualified as a girlfriend, so I didn't even look in her direction whenever I ran into her at the office, which wasn't often anyway.

One Friday night, I was on my way home and needed to drop some work off with Malcolm. Arriving at around nine, I found only Melanie at home, baby-sitting the children. I politely accepted the offer to stay for a drink, but purely out of courtesy, and because Melanie asked so nicely. She later told me that she was so desperate for adult conversation that she would have invited anybody in! During our conversation, I thought it a good opportunity to convey my faith to Melanie, whom I believed to be in need of it. I told her how difficult ethical aspects of my job were for me, and how as a Christian I found the line that I had to tow quite hard at times. To my surprise, she responded by saying that she could relate. I almost fell off my chair. At the same time, this made me sit up and take interest. The conversation wasn't bad, and as I was tired after a hard week, I found the good company soothing. Melanie ordered pizzas and insisted on paying, and we spend the best part of two hours together. As I left, I remembered my manners and offered to return the favor soon – trying to be the perfect gentleman.

Roughly a month later, I was working very late one Wednesday night before a public holiday, and got to the point where I had had enough. I thought the following day, being a public holiday, would be a good opportunity to return the favor by asking Melanie out. I promptly phoned Melanie and although she was busy the following night, she suggested we go out that Friday night, 25 September 1998. On Friday, Malcolm teased me, and said our 'date' spelled trouble, which I just laughed off. Melanie and I went to a pizzeria in Sandton, in the northern suburbs of Johannesburg, and I can still recall every moment of that evening. I fell hopelessly in love that night. As I got into my car after dropping her off at home, I uttered these words: 'Lord I don't know what this was, but, damn, this was good company.' Over the next weeks we went through the normal courting games. Melanie got cold feet, while I just couldn't bring myself to stop wanting to court her. Something about this girl just wouldn't let me give up!

Six weeks later, I sat Melanie down and told her that I could not continue with her like this. I explained that clearly I was in this relationship with the longer-term view of marriage, while she kept saying that she just wanted to be friends. If there is one thing that I did not have time for, it was a girl that I was in love with that just wanted to be friends. In fact, I was not dating or looking for love when I met Melanie – it just happened. I was enjoying my career immensely, and had resigned myself to the fact that if I never married, it would be perfectly fine with me. We broke up and I asked Melanie to please give me space and not have contact with me so that I could get over her. After all, I was in love with her. She did not oblige me! It wasn't even a week before I received a phone call from her. Her voice alone melted any resistance I might have had, and we plodded along for another month until early December, at which time I reiterated our situation to Melanie before leaving on holiday. I was so desperate to get over her that I gave Malcolm a number where he could reach me and switched off my mobile phone, the voicemail box and every other possible means by which Melanie could reach me. But a day later, I had rethought the situation, and during the long drive down to Cape Town, I phoned her. I told her that we could not continue as things were – her wanting to be friends, and me wanting more.

A couple of days later I had a call from Melanie. She was all alone in Johannesburg and desperately ill with glandular fever. I felt so sorry for her that I phoned her every day, arranged for flowers to be sent to her, and did my utmost to care for her. I was visiting Hugo on his farm in the

Cape, and the only good mobile phone reception was next to a small tree at the edge of his lawn. He still refers to the tree as the courting tree – because of the amount of time I spent under that tree that summer on the phone with Melanie! Yet Hugo knew me better than anybody, and he could see how the situation was tearing me apart. He took me up one of the hills overlooking the mountains, and we prayed together, as we had so often done in Stellenbosch. He told me that I needed to make a decision about Melanie, as I had come to stay with him to get over her, after all. I knew he was right and the next day I told Melanie that I had to break off contact with her again, and begged her to respect my wishes this time. I told her I would call her when I was ready. This was shortly before Christmas. It was very hard not to call Melanie on Christmas Day, especially since she was in the final recovery days of the fever. One morning, shortly after Christmas, I woke up with a crystal clear mind. I would go back to Jo'burg a week later, and tell Melanie one more time that I want to marry her. If she declined, I decided I would never see her again. After that, I didn't mind phoning her to chat, as I now had a plan. We spoke frequently, and as only people in love can. At midnight on 31 December, I called her to wish her a good year with her upcoming studies, and every other aspect of her life. I reached her voicemail and left a long message. She was at the midnight service, led by Alan Storey, and he was preaching on the theme of 'sliding doors.' Alan and Melanie had become good friends, and while they were both denying it, there were some romantic feelings between them. At a quarter past twelve that night, she called, and we chatted and then I went to bed.

As I woke up the next morning, I decided to switch my mobile phone on briefly. Four voice messages! The first one was a very serious message from Melanie at five past five that morning, saying she needed to talk to me urgently, and that she was flying down to Cape Town to do so! The second message was from her crazy friend Kym, shouting that Melanie wanted to marry me and I had better not mess it up! The third message was from Melanie's other friends informing me of her flight details, and pleading with me to be at the airport. As I was listening to the last voice message – someone just hanging up – my phone rang. It was Melanie. 'Are you kidding,' I asked. 'Would I kid about something like this?' she replied. That day was the most anxious and nervous day of my life; I must have gone to the bathroom every 20 minutes! After picking Melanie up from the airport, and a day spent together, with Melanie being 'mute', I finally confronted her about and why she was there. She looked at me all puzzled and said, 'You once said you wanted to marry me. I am here to say that I will.' And with that we were engaged. I gave her a ring only five months later in our church very early one morning. We had communion and sealed our engagement with a kiss. Exactly one year after our first date, on 25 September 1999, we were married.

This was against everything that I believed, and everything that I had ever stood for. During my last year at Stellenbosch, I was quite vocal about having relationships only with someone of the opposite sex with whom you shared a spiritual bond and that had a similar level of maturity in your faith. Rosemary Hack told me while Hermien and I were still together, that you should never marry anyone who doesn't share your vision. Melanie and I had not even prayed together before we got married. It was because I was in total denial, or because I knew our relationship was so right that the weight of my previous convictions held little weight. Of course, today I know it was the latter.

For me, being with Melanie was the most natural thing on earth. In the first couple of weeks after her surprising me, I caught myself being suspicious, and wondering whether she would get cold feet. She never did, and soon we settled into a relationship that resembled a married couple. From the first day, we shared everything: emotional wellbeing, finances and every other aspect of our lives. Ten years have since passed, and nothing has changed. We have had our own journeys of growth, but at the core, a fundamental love for each other and a deep knowledge of being each other's best friend has remained.

In the time that we have been together Melanie continues to surprise me, particularly with regard to her spiritual growth. While I came from a very astute and convicted Christian background, Melanie's faith is more practical. She has experienced God in very real ways, with little knowledge of the Bible, theology or any other source. For her, God was real because she could feel him. I was always astonished at her absence of knowledge, and even more so at her comfort with this absence.

I would lie if I said that we shared a great deal spiritually in the early days of our relationship. On the contrary, I can't remember ever praying together. Melanie had a need for that, and we tried once or twice to develop a weekly time together devoted to Bible study and prayer, but it just never worked for me. I suppose this was more due to my own feelings of alienation during the earlier days I spent in Johannesburg than a reflection on Melanie. We went to church every Sunday, and we would have long debates, agreeing or disagreeing, over what was taught. We shared much in our mutual growth of understanding and independent views as to where we felt the church and Christianity were wrong, and inevitably we shaped one another's views, as I suppose any married couple do.

As time went by, Melanie and I grew parallel on our views on Christianity, spiritualism, and religion, and those have never been out of sync longer than a few months. By this, I mean that even though one of us might have read a book, or been exposed to some literature, and arrived at some conclusion or changed our views, any differences in our outlook would never last longer than three months in general. The process is mutual and we continue to help each other grow. At the core of this lies the mutual respect we have for each other, and the willingness to listen to the new discoveries the other has made.

Melanie's influence is probably the single largest catalyst for my own process of consciousness, awakening, and subsequent liberation from religion. Although we were happily married by all standards, unbeknown to me Melanie was feeling very unhappy and unfulfilled. I was too unaware at the time to realize that I was not feeling fulfilled either, and believed that having a conflict-free relationship meant that we were happy (as opposed to other couples that were constantly fighting). Melanie, in her psychology studies, had come across Harville Hendrick's Imago relationship theory. Having read his book *Getting the Love You Want* (Hendrix, 1993), she was convinced that we needed to attend such a course. Not being a prohibitive kind of husband, I agreed. So, in December 2005 we attended an Imago course. It changed our lives. It transformed our marriage from a subconscious power struggle to a conscious partnership of two individuals seeking to fulfil the other's core needs daily. The course essentially makes you aware of the hurts in your partner's past, and how these translate into certain actions in everyday life.

In the process of unraveling these things, through a process designed by Hendricks, every individual becomes aware of underlying currents in his or her own emotional make-up, which translate to certain day-to-day actions. Many of these are conflict-evoking actions. I, for example, became aware how I continuously hurt Melanie by disappearing into an emotional silo. I do this subconsciously. Through the process, I discovered the reasons that I do this, and how I can receive healing from the reasons for my behavior.

While Imago changed our marriage, it also changed each of us individually. It offered us a stream of thought to work from, and placed both of us on a very aggressive growth path regarding our consciousness. Let me state that I don't believe there is a defined movement of consciousness, but that there is a whole field of study around aspects of life, which inevitably comes down to matters of consciousness. I am sometimes asked what I mean when I encourage people to be more conscious. Well, to begin with, being conscious is not the opposite of being knocked unconscious, that is, in physical terms. It refers more to acting emotionally and rationally from the rational section of your brain, namely the frontal lobe, and more specifically your cerebral cortex. It means not acting from your pre-historic 'reptile' brain, which acts purely on instinct, but rather to become aware of those forces happening inside of you, and then acting from the cerebral cortex. Without going into the theory too deeply, the only aspect I would like to highlight here is a higher state of awareness and therefore a higher state of consciousness. I think it is best described with an example:

Living in a big city, I used to be very prone to road rage. I discussed this in therapy and discovered that I mostly got irritated with drivers when they acted as if I wasn't there – pushing in front of me, passing me on the left,[43] or driving on my tail. I realized that this behavior evoked old childhood hurts of not being seen, of being treated as just one of the masses. As with the middle-child syndrome I had suffered when growing up in my family, always feeling as if I just blended in, without any special attention being given to me. I realized that this evoked a 'fear of invisibility' in me. Once I became aware of the underlying dynamic that made me act in stupid ways on the road, I was able to consciously decide to engage, or not to engage with particular drivers. Now when someone pushes in front of me, I remind myself (sometimes aloud) that I am not invisible, and that nothing a person does can make me invisible. I also place my attention on that driver, and try to understand why that person might push in front of me. From this premise, I am able to accept that the person has nothing to do with me, and that I can choose to act according to the pre-historic drivers from my 'reptile' brain that just want to defend, regardless of reason, or from a rational cerebral cortex point of view. The latter does not cost me energy, the former does, so in most cases I choose the latter.

I have managed to achieve this through higher awareness, and by placing my attention on certain key areas that I become aware of, which result in a higher state of consciousness. This is what I mean when I encourage people to be more conscious. Just to solidify the issue, I'll give another example. This time from my family life.

I used to hate going to events where I knew my parents, brother and sister would be. Somehow, I always ended up feeling all the emotions that I felt as a child, and that alone was enough to scare me away. With the help of Melanie, and subsequent therapy, I have been able to change that.

It first took Melanie to make me aware of how I change in my family's presence, as a result of the interpersonal dynamics playing out between us. I then analyzed what I felt and discovered this same 'fear of invisibility', which in this context did two things primarily. It wanted to show off my intellect with heavily armored rational arguments in the hope that my family would recognize how clever I was – all subconsciously, of course. Second, as nobody noticed this – because they were mostly all trying to do the same thing, particularly my siblings – I started to speak louder, and listen less. It should come as no surprise that this is also exactly what my parents and siblings did, so our family dinner table discussions mostly ended up being a very loud noise of people fighting subconsciously for position. Harville Hendrix's Imago therapy teaches about this precise need, and how one actively has to start listening for others to feel heard and understood. Sadly, my family does not always get that.

For about a year or two after first realizing this, I would be sucked into playing out old dynamics and behavior patterns in their presence, but the difference was that I wasn't just being pulled into a vortex. Now I knew what was happening to me, even though I could not stop it from happening. It was as if I had become aware of my own actions, without being able to stop myself from doing it. Sometimes, before I knew it, I had made some clever comment in order to be seen, and often I grew louder as the evening grew older, but it was different. With a little more work and more attention to the issue, with greater awareness every time we were together, I eventually reached a point where I could just observe the family dynamic. I now function at a higher state of consciousness around my family. Instead, now I witness and recognize the unconscious behavior of my parents and siblings, whereas before this would suck me into arguments and other negative behavior. I still feel the pull of wanting to do something to be seen or heard, but where it used to be an irresistible pull, it is now merely a slight tug – that I believe will be with me all my life. Being the master of my own actions is an incredibly liberating experience, and this is the result of living a more conscious life. This raised-awareness is what I try incorporate into my everyday life and it translates to what Echardt Tolle calls 'being in the now' (Tolle, *The Power of Now*, 1999).

Melanie and I have transformed our marriage through Imago therapy to become more conscious, yet the reality is that once you learn to act in such a manner toward your spouse, it is impossible to continue to live differently in other relationships. Sure, the safety and willingness to analyze oneself regarding conscious issues is not always reciprocated, but I find that I am less and less sucked into situations in my life where I act from premises other than my cerebral cortex. Before this starts to sound as if Imago is all about rational thought and no emotion, let me assure you it is quite the opposite. Once you are able to be aware of your own and your partner's dynamics and underlying pain and fears, you are able to engage with the emotions so much more – without being defensive about it. Your conscious awareness allows you to feel another's pain and joy, while still being aware that these are not your emotions. In this way, other people's emotions do not intimidate or overwhelm you, but rather you are able to share on an emphatic level, rather than re-living it. Only humans have this ability through our cerebral cortex. When dogs get scared because they are reminded of some negative emotion in their past, they do not have the conscious ability to discern that the danger is not real, and that their feelings are merely an echo of the original danger. Thus, they bark and show their teeth. My two border collies often bark at me at night when I arrive home. If they had a cerebral cortex and a higher consciousness, they would realize the danger is not real, even though they feel fear.

For me, it was as if someone had switched on the colour in my otherwise monochrome life. All the images were the same, but suddenly they were expressed more vividly and came more to life. Over time, the world of emotion had become part of my life, and I started to understand the language of emotion. I had a greater awareness of other people's fears, anxieties, joys, and happiness. I became more able to read my clients, colleagues, friends and family. Increasingly, I would become aware of another's fears, and act in a way to create safety, rather than evoke transference-patterns that would recreate the other's hurt. For the non-psychologically inclined out there, let me explain this. Imago states that we have a tendency to want to re-create situations from our childhood where we got hurt, in order to re-enact the circumstance with a hope of repairing our hurt and creating a better outcome. Sadly, while this happens in an subconscious way, most people achieve the re-enactment, but the result is the same, which causes even more hurt. Alas, people are caught in perpetual cycles of continuously re-enacting their childhood pain, never receiving any relief. Such is the world of unconscious behavior. Let me give another example from my own life.

One of my deepest pains as a child is that of not feeling special and loved. Regardless of whether I was loved or not (which I was), I somehow was wounded and therefore needed to heal this. I found myself in my adult life adopting the persona of being a 'nice guy.' Most people I dealt with would comment on what a nice guy I was. But behind the nice guy lay a subconscious need to be noticed (counteracting my fear of invisibility) and loved. While I received both on a superficial level, on a deeper level I did not. Nice guys have a tendency to blend in, because they are so amicable. Because I played the nice guy, clients would not answer e-mails and would miss appointments, believing that because 'he's such a nice guy, he'll understand.' Friends would not consider my needs because 'he's such a nice guy, he'll fall in with any plans.' These subtle recreations of my own continued to hurt me deep into my adult life. It is only our conscious awakening that allowed us to become more aware of these dynamics in all our relationships, and to start managing these in a safer and more loving way.

This liberation has evoked such a passion in me to become more aware, that everything I read these days is aimed at raising my awareness or gaining greater access to consciousness. I have become passionate about the subject of consciousness, and spend most of my idle hours exploring this further. You don't have to delve too deep into consciousness these days before you run into quantum physics, and for Melanie and me this opened up yet another level of understanding, which ultimately led to new views on religion and a further 'unchaining' of God. More about this though, in Chapter 8, "What the Bleep Did I Know?".

Chapter 7 *Church Alienation*

The absence of spiritual intimacy with God and Jesus that had crept into my life during my early days in Johannesburg had a different side to it. After listening to Landa Cope, my God was bigger and different from the God that I had heard other Christians speak or preach about. My God was like an engineer (for lack of a better description), and I had now glimpsed his blueprint, not just the results of it – to which I felt many other people's understanding being limited.

In every conversation I had, and in every context where I chose to engage in the subject with others, I felt alienated as a result of my views. I wasn't pushy and often disengaged very early in a conversation, but the resulting feeling was that of loneliness. Yes, I had Melanie who shared my views on God, and our views were shaped together and by one another. However, this was precisely the problem. I needed outside input, people who would challenge, and help to shape my path of growth. Melanie could contribute, but ultimately we were too close for her to challenge my views in any radical way, and vice versa.

And so, I grew increasingly lonely as a Christian. Numerous times I would meet somebody and we would build up a very good rapport in a short space of time, particularly around Christian matters. In me there would be this deep desire to share and engage in my views, and often we would set up appointments to do so. Sadly, every single time I started to feel safe enough to share my views, it evoked a response from the other person who, nine out of ten times, would want to help me find the 'right way' again. Too many of these individuals left, never making contact with me again, and avoiding any contact I tried to make. I often wondered what it was about my views that are so alienating – views on the objective of Christianity not being salvation, but of living a life of higher purpose, which would bring about the kingdom of God. Views such as the church having got it all wrong, and having created a dichotomy between right and wrong, good and bad. Views that it wasn't always like this, but had only started to appear in church literature around the 1850s. Views that a non-believing surgeon performing heart surgery can be busy with work that is as holy in God's kingdom as a minister baptizing a child; that each of us are given certain talents with which to fulfill our purpose, of which the church is but one. Views that fulfilling your God-ordained purpose could be done in isolation from the church, that going to church and tithing do not per se sanctify my secular existence. Furthermore, views that the church does not stand in opposition to the secular, and that the church is the only place where this separation is upheld. Are these thoughts so radical as to alienate most Christians? It seems so. In fact, most Christians that I spoke to were glad to accept some of these thoughts, but eventually they just became too threatening to their faith. One could almost mark the moment when the 'shutters went down', and these people stopped listening, from which point onwards their only objective was to convert me back to 'the right path.' There was one person however, with whom I did not feel this alienation. Someone who I always felt understood what I was saying. This was Alan Storey.

Alan is the son of the famous anti-apartheid church leader and now lecturer at Duke University, Peter Storey. Alan is an amazing man. I don't have more respect for anybody in this world, with regard to his conviction, clarity of thought, and braveness to explore. Alan was tormented as a child for his father's convictions, and learned to keep his hands in his pockets when bullied by older boys, because non-violence is a very strong conviction of his. He was later prosecuted for opposing the apartheid military conscription, and was labeled a political activist by the regime. Alan is a man who boldly speaks his truth, regardless of consequence, and lives this truth with an integrity that I have not seen in others.

I met Alan in the strangest way possible. Whether it is true or not, it was my perception that Alan and Melanie were in the early stages of falling love with each other when I came into the picture. Melanie was heavily involved with the church, and was designated to show the new minister around the congregation of Calvary Methodist Church, in Midrand, Johannesburg. They spent a lot of official time together, and I soon became aware that this man was as much a part of Melanie's unwillingness to be in a relationship with me, as were her own fears. While never having dated, there was some electricity between them, and it was tangible, even to me. Melanie might have denied it, but I knew about Alan. At the same time, I could see that this was tormenting Melanie and decided to do something about it. I was determined to do the right thing, and decided I would go and meet this chap.

Not wanting Melanie's consent, as I thought this was a private matter, I drove to Midrand to the street where I remembered Melanie had said the church was. On reaching the church, I called the telephone number on the board. Not knowing who I was, or what my visit was about, Alan was willing to see me in his office. As I walked in, I told him that I was there because of our mutual friend Melanie, and that it was incredibly hard for her to be pursued by two men, and that I could see that it was tearing her to bits. 'I am here,' I told him, 'to ask for a period of truce for Melanie to make up her mind as to which of us she would like to see.' I went on to communicate that I was quite willing to walk away if Melanie chose Alan over me, but that I needed to know that she had the necessary space to make her decision. I felt it would be unfair if I gave her space, while Alan continued to see her.

Well, Alan almost fell off his chair in disbelief. He told me that he had no such intentions with Melanie, and that even if he had, he would never date anyone in his congregation. He thanked me for my honesty, and told me that I must have him confused with someone else. He asked me to join him in prayer for Melanie, and wished me good-bye. I left confused, feeling like a fool, and knowing that I was in deep trouble with Melanie! Yet, I suspected that I had gained Alan's respect that day – respect that would be reciprocated towards him in years to come. Shortly after Melanie visited me in Cape Town, she took me to a Saturday morning prayer meeting, so that her church friends could meet me – 'the mystery man.' Alan was there and from his attitude towards me, I saw both the respect and appreciation for the love that Melanie and I shared. It was a privilege to have Alan marry Melanie and me later that year.

After a year of not feeling rooted in a Christian community, I became a member of Calvary. This started a journey for me that would shape my Christian faith significantly. Alan is the most amazing preacher I have ever listened to; that includes his father, and Billy Graham, and Landa Cope. He has the ability to scrutinize the text, and through deep insight into the messages and meaning of the texts, he is able to communicate those clearly and in a challenging manner, if needed. I think part of his power as a preacher is the integrity with which he is willing to listen to the text himself, and act on this insight, irrespective of consequences. Few preachers actually 'walk the talk' and Alan only knows that way. He once told me that he tries to place himself inside the text to see what it is telling him, and often it tells him stuff about his own life that he does not want to hear. He then battles with himself first (often the night before the sermon), in order to walk onto the pulpit totally at peace with what the text is asking of him. From this premise, he can then share his insight with the congregation. This is bravery such as few others have. Most preachers would consciously or subconsciously shy away from aspects of the text that made them uncomfortable, but not Alan.

It was as if I had enrolled in a Christian understanding school during my theology schooling, had attended high school through listening to Landa Cope, and had now finally enrolled for university. Alan's insight into the Bible and Christianity could not have been better placed along my own development journey, even if I had planned it that way. There is so much that I learned from Alan, but fundamentally, he shifted my thinking around a couple of key issues regarding God. The most fundamental was that of God's inclusivity. Before you sigh with disbelief – because God's inclusivity is so central to the Christian faith that this is hardly any new insight – let me take you on a short journey to illustrate just how that so-called knowledge is interpreted by the modern church.

One of the earliest insights from Alan was around Jesus and his crucifixion. Alan postulated that God did not send his only son to die on the cross, but this was a by-product of him living the life he had to come to live. 'A God of love does not use evil as a means to achieve his goals' seems such an obvious insight to have, but the implications are rife. Jesus was crucified in the most cruel and inhumane way possible. There is nothing about the way in which he was tortured, and later killed, that speaks of the love of those who did it to him. On the contrary, much of what he had to endure was based on hatred and contempt. Would God have chosen evil-doers to achieve his means? Does this sound like an all-loving God? Does an almighty God need to use ways that contrast with his being, to achieve his means? Wasn't Jesus just murdered by the order of the day? Alan postulated that Jesus' mission was to come and live God's love for the world in concrete terms. Jesus was to live God's inclusivity, irrespective of the consequences. God was not to interfere with Jesus' life, and only asked Jesus to live with total love and total inclusivity. You will not find any contradiction to God's character of love in anything that Jesus did, even when he overturned the traders' tables in the temple – even then he was acting against the exclusivity of conditions (buy an offering) being laid down to gain access to God's love and mercy. The result? The order of the day, mostly the Jewish political leaders hated his message. Their power lay in the fact that God was in the temple and that they alone held the keys to gain access to God. They were the spiritual and political leaders, and through them God could be accessed. This smells of a political regime and Jesus' life challenged this. The masses were hearing Jesus' message that God's love is for all, and available to all, at all times. This undermined the political powers, and they were adamant that they must do something about it. Hence, they plotted to kill Jesus and carefully executed the plan. According to the Bible, Jesus, knowing what would happen to him, continued to live this life of love and inclusivity where all have equal access to God, and in the hours before his crucifixion he even prayed to God to ask whether this terrible consequence could be spared. Jesus was murdered.

To the church, Jesus came to save us from our sins as stated in John 3:16,[44] but if you read it carefully, it says nothing about dying or being sent to die. The church has conveniently implied that over time – since he met his death in such a terrible way. There is no reference in the gospels that Jesus came to die – you may find it in Paul's letters, but not in the gospels. The books are full of reference to Jesus' divinity, but nothing of this being his mission. In fact, I think Jesus summarizes his own mission quite well in John 17. This in itself is a can of worms, as the gospel of John was written many years after Jesus' death, so an actual account is highly questionable.[45]

The point is this: you need careful analysis of the actual text; an open-mind; and a willingness to deviate from mainstream church thinking to make bold statements such as Alan made continuously. At the same time, he was equipping me with a more liberal view of the world, and shaping my theology in a very profound way. While doing so, those who had thought me alien for my views before I met Alan, now thought outright that I was being blasphemous (which I have been accused of regularly).

There is another vital component of my Christian education, which Alan contributed to. Daniel Erlander wrote a book called *Manna & Mercy* (1992), which by my reckoning became Alan's credo. In fact, if you Google the title, you will find an equal number of references to Erlander and to Alan and his retreats, based on the book. The book simply illustrates how, throughout the history of the Jewish faith (Old Testament) and Christian faith (New Testament), there is one common theme: God has always provided in abundance, both materially (manna) and emotionally and spiritually (mercy). Throughout the ages, people have attempted to hoard these provisions, or control them for their own benefit. Every time this happened, people suffered, but in most cases, the hoarders or people of power suffered as much as their victims. From what I know today, this universal truth stretches far beyond Christianity or any faith. The universe is at a fundamental level is only energy, and energy can be neither created nor destroyed. The laws of the universe are such that there is abundance for all living things – it is only our species that takes more than it can consume, and lives with the fear that there will not be enough of what we need. So, we abuse the planet and grab more than we need, at the expense of others and the earth at large.

The thing that really changed my thinking about the message in *Manna & Mercy* is how God's grace is available to all unconditionally. You might argue that this is not an earth-shattering truth, but think again. I am suggesting that there are no conditions. In other words, I don't have to believe in Jesus; nor do I have to accept him. God gives his mercy irrespective of my position toward him. None of the conditions that the church informally suggests, or even sometimes strictly defines, apply. I need not pray, read the Bible, tithe, go to church, be kind, or believe any other dogmatic principle on which most churches are built. God gives his manna and mercy to each of us unconditionally.[46] A beautiful example is the love that a three-year-old girl shows when bringing her mother a flower. It is undeniable that this is love. So, if she has love in her and God is love, surely God is in her. A three-year old girl has little formalized concept of God, and has no way of 'accepting Jesus' at such a young age, as defined by Christianity.[47] If God can be present even in those who have not accepted him, surely his love is then available to all, irrespective of their stance towards him. There is love all over the world, visible and tangible, even from those who do not accept Jesus or God. Many humanitarians, without Jesus as their Savior, are far more compassionate than most Christians I know. The only way to get around this argument is to deny that God is love and love is God. This becomes a clearly defined difference, at which point I will not argue any further. My point of departure continues to be that: God is love and where love is, there is God.

If you want to challenge this dogma even further, you have to ask yourself this question: Will a God of love set any conditions to obtain his love? Human parents love their children, irrespective of the response they get from their children. Surely, God does too? Then when you throw out the argument of a jealous God who has to be feared, as read about in the Old Testament, I suggest you first read *Manna & Mercy* and spend some time considering the context of the Old Testament. Even if you choose to accept the God of the Old Testament, you can't deny that Jesus came and redefined this position toward one of 'love only.' Finally, you might accept that God gives his love freely, but in order to gain access to eternal communion with him, you have to accept Jesus as Savior. In this case, I would ask whether a loving God could be a conditional God? My aim is not to convince any reader of my viewpoint, but to give insight into the arguments that lead me to my own conclusions.

Regardless, Alan's passionate presentation of *Manna & Mercy* contributed immensely to my own thinking about the church. It challenged my thoughts like hardly any other literature has, and has given me a stillpoint from which to evaluate all future experiences of God, teachings about God, or any other matter pertinent to God. This stillpoint is simple: God is love. This was not new in my thinking, but its implications now had new meaning. More importantly, the examples in the Bible where people did not honor this stillpoint, and consequently damaged or hurt other people, are numerous. I realized then that there was such consistency in God and his love that it is almost too overwhelming for humanity to embrace. We somehow want to place restrictions (or conditions) on his love.

It's ironic that after my own separation from the Christian church, I have come across this notion in so many spiritual writings. It seems that many spiritual dogmas from many religions eventually reduce to one simple truth: God is love or compassion, or the universe is built from love, or the essence of the universe is compassion. It's interesting that in the book by Masaru Emoto, *The Hidden Messages of Water* (2001), even water responds best, at a crystal level, to feelings of love and gratitude. It means that I had stumbled upon a universal truth in *Manna & Mercy*, which would alienate me further from the formal church, and eventually bring me to the decision to break away from formal religion.

Alan also opened my mind to the possibility that Christianity is not the only way to God. I am not sure whether this was intentional, but I do know that he was deeply moved by some interactions he had with some Muslim people in Durban. I remember his sermon being vague about the issue, yet implying that our judgment of other faiths was loveless and not in alignment with the stillpoint of God as love. I spoke to him briefly after that sermon, and without asking him directly, I was fishing to figure out his views on whether in his mind Jesus was still the 'the way, the truth and the life.'[48] The implication of this is profound. If Muslims can have access to God without Jesus, then why am I a Christian? Moreover, from the premise of God's inclusivity, there is no reason that Muslims cannot have access to God in the same way as Christians, and therefore, it is quite possible that both Christians and Muslims are neither right nor wrong. To be honest, I think I wasn't ready to embrace the implication of this type of reasoning, and continued to choose to be a Christian even though at the core, I had no grounds to choose it over any other religion. In essence, I told myself that this is a choice of convenience since Christianity is what I know and understand, and I may as well be choosing Islam. It's important to remember that I had long forsaken the notion of Hell or condemnation, and while I still subscribed somewhat to the notion of Heaven, it really only meant permanent communion with God. Thus achieving this communion was now perfectly feasible through Islam as well, while I chose to be a Christian purely on the grounds of feeling that I had a relationship with Jesus and that my love for Jesus was why I remained a Christian.

Alan became a dear friend to Melanie and me, even though he is an elusive character to pin down for social interactions. Alan and I have had only a few breakfasts together over the past ten years. I am not always sure that my presence meant as much to him as his did to me, and it really didn't matter to me. I have often said to him that I think he is a prophet who is not yet recognized in his own time or country.

Throughout my time with Calvary, I had this overriding sentiment that the church was getting it wrong. I often challenged Alan on those aspects of his sermons where I felt the church was too judgmental about the secular world. My views that the separation between secular and holy did not exist meant that every time businesspeople were challenged to be more involved in the church, it would get my hackles up. I felt this was not what God intended, and that my own and other business people's sanctity (for want of a better word) did not lie in our sharing our skills with the church, tithing, or being involved in the church in any way or form. I stressed very often that Alan should be more sensitive to, and commend people to be the best that they can be in their chosen profession, irrespective of their involvement and contribution towards the church. While I knew Alan understood the inclusivity concept very well, I wasn't always convinced that he was as passionate about this point as I was. Even so, in this context, I felt alienated from Calvary, let alone the mainstream church.

I have accepted over time that I am a loner with regard to the church and most of its members, and have stopped engaging with people in order to share my views, or to find some communion with fellow Christians. In fact, I increasingly stopped sharing my views with most family and friends, as the net results were mostly just alienation, rather than an open-minded willingness to listen. If there is one topic where people in general are very defensive and unwilling to be open-minded, it is about issues of their faith, and, by implication, the particular franchise of the religion to which they subscribe.

And so, while I was a worship-leading member of Calvary for five years, and, by all accounts, an active member of the church, at the core it was only Alan Storey's incredible gift that kept me going back. Over time, as Calvary grew and employed more ministers so that Alan did not preach every week, it became a bit of a hit-and-miss scenario as to whether we would drive the 25 km to go to church, only to be bored to death by the sermon. Melanie always enjoyed going, as this was the church in which she grew up, so the social component of seeing her friends and friends of the family always made the trip worthwhile for her, but for me it increasingly became an effort to go to church, as I received very little from it. There is an old Christian saying that the church is not what you receive, but what you give, but even on that score, what I had to give brought little satisfaction or fulfillment. Our church was undergoing a dramatic culture change, from a predominantly white-English community to a predominantly black-African community. This in itself was a good thing and very inclusive by nature, but the cultural difference made for some severe differences in opinion about punctuality at worship team practices, the types of songs we sang, and the general liturgy of the service. In essence, I felt severely alienated by the Calvary community.

I gradually stopped attending church so that by 2006 I may have only attended once or twice a year. I had become quite an active cyclist, and it was very convenient to have cycling training on Sunday morning (which I loved) rather than be frustrated at church.

Chapter 8 *What the Bleep Did I Know?*

The documentary movie *What the Bleep Do We Know?* (Chasse, Vicente & Arntz, 2004) needs little introduction. It has become a cult film, and has had enormous success globally on a shoestring budget, mainly due to the effective word-of-mouth exposure it receives. If I had watched this movie any earlier than I did, it might not have been so fascinating. As it turns out, like so many things in my journey, I watched this movie with Melanie at a time that I was perfectly ready to hear what it had to say.

First, I have always had a fascination with quantum physics, and while I had little exposure to the concepts before *What the Bleep Do We Know? (WTB)*, I understood enough to know that it was radical. As an engineer, I have an above-average understanding of classical physics, particularly Newtonian movement physics. All I knew before *WTB* is that quantum physics is radically different from Newtonian physics. The movie by all accounts is a good introduction to quantum physics, and the microbiological and subsequent spiritual implications. It touches on areas such as 'the observer', and some of the more serious 'consciousness' questions. For me, it introduced me to a whole host of authors in the field of consciousness, many of whom have very diverse views. For example, Stuart Hamerhoff[49] is a pure scientist who provides quantum physical answers for just about everything, including near-death experiences, while Ramtha[50] is probably on the opposite side of that spectrum, being channeled through J Z Knight in the movie, and almost exclusively offers metaphysical explanations. Owing to time constraints in the movie, these authors have very little time to give an account of their worldview or any deeper explanation of the theories underlying their comments. I have, however, in further studies through their books and video documentaries with these and other authors researched the issues around consciousness much more deeply than the level presented in *WTB*.

This documentary set Melanie and me on an investigation into consciousness-related matters that changed us forever. At first, we watched *WTB* probably five times just to try to get to grips with the immense implications that the concepts in the film have on our everyday life. Every time we told friends about it, and invited them to watch it with us, we learned something new and understood concepts so much better. There were so many new concepts: the collapse of the wave function and parallel universes; being in infinitely many places at once; creating our own day daily; the inability of the brain to distinguish between thought and reality; how our senses deceive us; how the observer is influenced by mental limitations; who God is; and what God is; to highlight just a few.

At the heart of quantum physics is the dualistic nature of a light particle or photon. Newtonian physics tells us that light is both a particle – a photon that looks like and acts exactly like an electron – and a wave that looks like, and acts exactly like any other electro-magnetic wave, such as microwaves, and X-rays. Then in the 1920s, a physicist called Louis de Broglie asked why this dualistic nature is not true of ordinary matter, such as electrons, and he continued to postulate that this should be true. This dualistic nature puzzled physicists for a long time, until Einstein's general relativity theory opened the door to the emergence of quantum physics. Ironically Einstein did not completely subscribe to the theory and was in an endless debate with Neils Bohr over the topic.

The famous double-slit experiment[51] illustrated that a single electron passes through a double-slit simultaneously, creating an interference pattern on the other side, similar to that created by two-wave sources, in most cases, light sources. This was remarkable for a piece of matter – an electron was causing similar results to that of two waves. There was only one conclusion – the single electron went through both slits at the same time, and interfered with itself to form the wave pattern. Scientists then thought that if they placed an observing or measuring device at the slits, they should be able to measure which slit it actually went through. On doing the same experiment with the observing device, the electron behaved like a piece of matter (a marble for example) and did not create the interference pattern associated with waves. The conclusion: the electron was in super-position of infinite possibilities when not observed, which allowed it to go through two slits at the same time. As soon as it was observed, it collapsed to one of those possibilities and went through only one slit. The simple act of observing had changed the nature of the outcome of the experiment.

What did we learn from it? The implications are infinite. Start with your own body and consider the amount of electrons in your body at any given time. Then consider that these electrons are in infinite super-positions; consider further that you as the observer are responsible for those super-positions to collapse into one of its infinite possibilities on a continuous basis. Scientists have not quite worked out how this works in our everyday life, but we know on a quantum level that being observed changes the physical universe.

That is the exact point where the physical and the metaphysical meet. Popular publications such as *The Secret* (Byrne, 2006) declare that you can create your own reality and you do so by placing your immediate and continuous attention on whatever it is that you want to materialize. Concrete studies proving this ancient meta-physical notion are still lacking, but it does correlate with what we now know happens on a quantum level, namely that when you observe or put your attention on something, it changes purely because of your attention and one of an infinite amount of possibilities materializes.

The best-selling authors of *The Art of Possibility* (2000), Benjamin and Rosamund Zander, visited South Africa not too long ago to present what is in essence a three-hour seminar of their book. As Ben said in his entertaining talk during the seminar: 'This is not a motivational talk, but a transformational talk.' What I found interesting is that Ben and Roz, completely oblivious of quantum physical theories or any knowledge of the collapse of the wave function, stumbled upon this truth as the result years of careful observation of Roz's work as a counseling psychologist and Ben's work as a conductor of the Boston Philharmonic Orchestra and artistic director of the music programme at Walnut Hill, a high school for the performing arts in Boston. They discovered that life has infinite possibilities, and as long as you allow yourself to be open to any possibility, any possibility was indeed possible. In fact, Roz discovered that if you tell yourself the story of your future the way that you like it, this story will most likely materialize. As soon as you use words such as 'can't', 'won't', 'right', 'wrong', 'impossible' and other limiting words, you are excluding certain possibilities from your reality. To me, this just sounds like a multitude of wave functions of matter in permanent super-position, collapsing in a predictable pattern based on the associated attention (either positive or negative) given to it. In fact, metaphysical literature such as *The Secret* suggests the 'law of attraction', which simply states that whatever you put your attention on, you will attract. In this way, accident-prone individuals continue to attract accidents, based on their continual expectations of them, while people born with silver spoons in their mouths continuously have all the luck in the world because that is their expectation. Again, at a quantum physical level the collapse of the wave function seems to be the physical explanation for what the metaphysical field has attached to 'mysterious forces.'[52]

Essentially, what this alludes to is the notion of parallel universes and that the scientific world is conjecturing on this matter more than anything else is. There is, however, reference in *WTB* to the electrons in our universe that pop in and out of existence in the super-position wave function, which raises the questions: where do these electrons disappear to, and where do they reappear from? It raises the question of the possibility of parallel universes (in fact an infinite amount of parallel universes) very strongly.

Moving across to a completely metaphysical field, in his book *Journey of Souls* (1994), Michael Newton explains that before souls incarnate, they investigate the lives they are about to enter, and look at the various decisions that they need to make in order to fulfill the karmic lessons they wish to learn in this particular lifetime. In my mind, I see many parallel lines with dots acting as decision-making nodes. At each decision-making node, we choose particular decisions (from an infinite amount of possibilities as per the wave function and 'art of possibility'). As we make these decisions, we jump from one universe to another, as these particular decisions, and the associated attention we give them, allow the wave function to collapse into one of the parallel possibilities or universes.

Of course, the collapse of the wave function raises an infinite amount of philosophical questions. For instance, if all my electrons are in super-position and only collapse when observed or attention is placed on them, then technically I am everywhere at once, yet physically I am only where I am when I am aware of my own physical presence or of being observed. There is a famous paradox illustrating this problem very well, referred to as the 'Schrödinger's cat paradox.' In this thought experiment, and in simple terms, Schrödinger postulated that if he had a cat in a box with a deadly poison that was activated when an electron passed through one slit of the double slit experiment, and not activated when it passed through the other, a paradox manifests itself. The electron, as per the double slit experiment, then passes through both slits when not observed, both activating and not activating the poison. This means that the cat in the box is both dead and alive at the same time. Only when the box is opened, and the cat is observed, will the wave function collapse to one of these possibilities and only then will the observer discover whether the cat is indeed alive or dead. Logically this is absurd, yet philosophically this illustrates how strange the quantum world, and by implication the universe we occupy, really is.

What is the spiritual implication of all of this? Well, from a traditional Christian point of view, the mere thought of being able to influence my own destiny, or create my own reality merely by observing, borders on the blasphemous, if it isn't already. The willingness to regard the universe as fluid, while every moment is a manifestation of some aspect of some parallel universe, leaves less and less space for a creator God with divinely ordained destinies for every human being. I am not suggesting that *WTB* and Christianity are on a direct collision course, but the notions covered in the film and the subsequent material I have read are not exactly mainstream Christianity. If I had not been alienated for my theological views, these not-so-Christian views did not make life any easier. For me, there was no conflict, and I could reconcile my theology perfectly with the quantum world. If anything, my awe for a higher intelligent being continued to increase on understanding the details that *WTB* illustrated.

There were some interesting discoveries in *WTB* too. One is that the senses we rely on so heavily are not in reality very reliable. In fact, our senses are really a function of our evolutionary development and pretty much a function of what we need to survive as a species – nothing more and nothing less. Again, Roz Zander came to a similar realization, from a much more practical perspective, by the following experiment conducted in the 1950s:

> A now-classic 1953 experiment revealed to stunned researchers that a frog's eye is capable of perceiving only four types of phenomena:
>
> - Clear lines of contrast
> - Sudden changes in illumination
> - Outlines in motion
> - Curves of outlines of small, dark objects
>
> A frog does not 'see' its mother's face, it cannot appreciate a sunset, or the nuances of color. It 'sees' only what it needs to see, in order to eat and to avoid being eaten: small, tasty bugs, or the sudden movement of a stork coming in its direction. The frog's eye delivers extremely selective information to the frog's brain. The frog perceives only what fits into its hardwired categories of perception.
>
> Human eyes are selective, too, though magnitudes more complex than those of the frog. We think we can see 'everything' until we remember that bees make out patterns written in ultraviolet light on flowers, and owls see in the dark. The senses of every species are fine-tuned to perceive information critical to their survival – dogs hear sounds above our range of hearing, insects pick up molecular traces emitted from potential mates acres away.

> We *perceive* only the sensations we are programmed to receive, and our awareness is further restricted by the fact that we *recognize* only those for which we have mental maps or categories. (Zander, 2000, p. 10)

A similar notion is outlined in *WTB*. Legend has it that when Christopher Columbus approached the Americas and the West Indies, the inhabitants were unable to physically see his ships approaching. The concept, or category, as Roz Zander defines it, had not yet been defined. The inhabitants could 'see' the disturbances in the water caused by the boats, but not the boats themselves. It was only when the shaman stared at the water long enough, no doubt with an open mind, that he or she was able to 'see' the ships. Once the shaman saw the ships, he or she was able to create the mental map or open the category that allowed all inhabitants to see the ships too. The really intriguing things, though, for modern-day inhabitants particularly of post-modern Western societies, are the questions: What other mental maps or categories are unavailable to us? What other realities are we not aware of, purely because our senses are not perceiving these realities? Ask yourself this question as you read this book: Am I static, or am I moving? What do my senses tell me?[53] Provided you are not on some sort of transport, your answer to the first question will most likely be – yes, I am static. Yet, you are moving at blistering speeds through space, via the earth's rotation around its own axis, and around the sun – your senses deceive you completely. By the same token, your senses tell you that you are operating on a flat earth, yet we know the earth to be round.

Another amazing example of the selectiveness of our senses is the recent experiment done jointly between the *Washington Post* and world-famous violinist Joshua Bell. Two weeks before the experiment, Bell had filled the house at Boston's stately Symphony Hall, where average seats went for

$100. The experiment was conducted during rush hour in a Washington underground station. The purpose of the experiment was to ascertain whether people could recognize beauty and brilliance in unexpected places and times (Weingarten, 2007).[54] In the experiment, Bell played some of the most difficult violin music ever composed, while busking for a period of 43 minutes, and was observed by 1 097 people. It took three minutes for anybody to notice, and during the whole time only six people stopped to listen while he earned $32,17 for his efforts from public contributions (one contributor gave $20). There are many conclusions one can come to, but the obvious question is this: If those 1 000 people had known what they were presented with, if their categories for observation and awareness had been opened, would they have responded in the same fashion? In addition, if such beauty and brilliance can go unnoticed, what else are we not noticing in our busy everyday lives?

What is the meaning of this in a spiritual context? Through the ages, humanity has attributed supernatural and mystical explanations to experiences their senses detected, but which they could not explain. Every society from every civilization has arrived – at some time – at some concept of God, which helped them to explain what they could not understand. Quantum mechanics places a large question mark over the observable universe, which by implication places a large question mark over the mystical explanations of our ancestors. This alone is not sufficient to disregard God as a concept. It does, however, beg some attention and the willingness to approach the concept of God afresh. It would be negligent of me not to include the sceptical view of what I am alluding to. There is definitely not concrete proof of a clear connection between quantum mechanics and consciousness (Carrol, 1994–2009).[55] I include as an end note a reference to a 20-year-old letter, which the sceptics like to hang onto, and which makes a compelling case. Read it and make up your own mind.[56] I am aware that anything metaphysical can be challenged by traditional science, which is why I am happy to entertain the views of the strictly scientific must-see-to-believe society. I would just like to remind those coming at this topic with a strong pragmatic approach that the Einstein's general relativity theory was not proven for many years after it was conjectured and Freud's concept of a subconscious took years before it was recognized by mainstream science. Sometimes scientists are a little too quick to discard new thought patterns, purely because there is no concrete evidence. Suffice it to say, the fields of consciousness and quantum mechanics have moved much closer in the past decade, so much so that I am convinced that the concrete proof that sceptics dismiss is closer than it was in 1986 (when the letter was written) and much closer than we all think.

One of the more striking questions in *WTB* regarded the identity of 'the observer.' This might sound like an obvious question, but on a deeper level, the question is more profound than meets the eye. Eckhart Tolle, author of the best-selling books *A New Earth* (2005) and *The Power of Now* (1999, p. 1), tells how he reached a point in his life when he wanted to commit suicide. While contemplating the act, he said to himself that he had reached a point where he could no longer live with himself. At that moment, he had an epiphany: 'Am I one or two? If I cannot live with myself, there must be two of me: the "I" and the "self" that "I" cannot live with' (Tolle, 1999, p. 1). Which of these two entities is his true self and which is not? His books are witness that Eckhart had discovered 'the observer' and from that point onwards was able to discern that he is more than his material body, and what he called 'self' was more than the mind where the ego resides. In a seminar that I attended by Deepak Chopra, best-selling author of numerous books, he explained that our body is physically rejuvenated (cell replacement) several times in a month and as we breathe, we breathe out molecules that were once a part of our livers, hearts, brains, kidneys and every other part of our bodies. At the same time, we inhale molecules that were part of other living organisms so that it is impossible to find an identity in the physical human body. He used the example of a neuro-scientist, who had found the connecting nerves that controlled a subject's motor-actions in his arm so that he could take over complete control of the subject's arm. He then told the subject, who now had no neurological connection with his arm, to move his arm in front of his face, while the scientist was giving the arm the command to move above his head. To his astonishment, the subject was able to control the arm, although no neurological signals could connect his brain to his arm. Deepak poses the question: Who was it then controlling the arm? As he puts it: 'We know where the command centre is, but who is the commander?' There is such significance in this notion of 'the observer' and 'consciousness.' Like a computer, human beings are wired, but something other than the wires is controlling the wires – what is that something and who is that something? This is the ultimate question in consciousness.

Slowly but surely, quantum mechanics and the parallel metaphysical associations were starting to give some logical explanation for what humanity had attributed to God over the centuries. Granted, hardly any of the metaphysical deductions could be proven, but, as I pointed out, there is at least some grounding in it that is possible to prove at this stage. If I was going to believe in something, I would rather believe in something that has the possibility of being proven and has some logical foundations than what had already been proved unlikely. My explorations of the quantum world were increasingly giving me alternative answers to the mystical answers about God and Jesus that I had grown up with. Increasingly, what people attributed to the work of God became mere logical explanations in the quantum world, albeit that a fair amount of conjecture and hypothesizing accompanied my reasoning. Still, I had a greater resonance with the quantum conjectures than with the notion of blind faith, which is based on nothing but mysticism. Like so many times in my journey, the next serious crossroad in my life came at exactly the right time. This in itself is a religious paradox, as I could choose to attribute this timing to the work of God or I could seek more scientific reasons that every step of my journey has had such perfect timing. This choice is often the difference between blind-faith believers and me. I have always chosen to challenge God, to allow myself greater insight into the mystical workings, rather than merely accept something in blind faith.

Chapter 9 *Losing Jesus*

As life goes, my spiritual growth ebbed and flowed, so that there was a period of consolidation in my mind as these newly discovered truths settled in my make-up. None of these challenged my Christian belief system, but happened parallel to the growth, based on *Manna & Mercy* and the teachings from Alan's sermons.

As time went on, these highly controversial concepts started to settle in me and became part of my everyday life. My quest to understand God shifted away from the realm of quantum physics toward the dichotomies between the church and my stillpoint for God. It was at this time that I stumbled on the book by Timothy Freke and Peter Gandy called *The Jesus Mysteries* (2001) – a controversial book, as one would expect from any book that claims Jesus had no historical authenticity. On a South African pay-channel, I watched a journalistic programme, *Carte Blanche,* which discussed the book and interviewed the authors. I bought the book because of the back cover, and the curiosity the questions raised in me:

What if:

- There was absolutely no evidence for the existence of a historical Jesus?
- For thousands of years, pagans have also followed a Son of God?
- This pagan savior was also born on twenty-fifth December before three shepherds; turned water into wine at a wedding; died and was resurrected; and offered his body and blood as Holy Communion?

- These pagan myths had been re-written as the gospel of Jesus Christ?

- The earliest Gnostic Christians knew that the Jesus story was a myth?

- Christianity turned out to be a continuation of paganism by another name? (Freke and Gandy, 2001, backcover)

This alone was enough to make me sit up and give attention. From the opening pages, Freke and Gandy make a compelling case:

> Where today the gathered faithful revere their Lord Jesus Christ, the ancients worshiped another god-man who, like Jesus, had been miraculously born on December 25 before three shepherds. In this ancient sanctuary, Pagan congregations once glorified a Pagan redeemer who like Jesus, was said to have ascended and to have promised to come again at the end of time to judge the quick and the dead. On the same spot where the Pope celebrates the Catholic mass, Pagan priests also celebrated a symbolic meal of bread and wine in memory of their savior who, just like Jesus, had declared:
>
> 'He who will not eat of my body and drink of my blood, so that he will be made one with me and I with him, the same shall not know salvation.'
>
> When we began to uncover such extraordinary similarities between the story of Jesus and Pagan myth we were stunned. We had been brought up in a culture that portrays Paganism and Christianity as entirely antagonistic religious perspectives. How could such astonishing resemblances be explained? We were intrigued and began to search farther. The more we looked, the more resemblances we found. To account for the wealth of evidence we were unearthing, we felt compelled to completely review our understanding of the relationship between Paganism and Christianity, to question beliefs that we previously regarded as unquestionable and to imagine possibilities that at first seemed impossible. Some readers will find our conclusions shocking and

> others heretical, but for us they are merely the simplest and most obvious way of accounting for the evidence we have amassed.
>
> We have become convinced that the story of Jesus is not the biography of a historical Messiah, but a myth based on perennial Pagan stories. Christianity was not a new and unique revelation but actually a Jewish adaptation of the ancient Pagan Mystery religion. This is what we have called The Jesus Mysteries Thesis. (Freke & Gandy, 2001, p 1)

Whether you accept the hypothesis posed by the book or not, it really is a fascinating argument and a book well worth reading. The excerpt I quote above is just the hook. Later in the book, the authors explain that these pagan faiths – with the startling similarities to Jesus' story – had been practised for centuries before the historical date of Jesus. The thesis continues to suggest that the Jewish religion had been under threat from other religions, and that a mythical figure had to be found for their religion, which could compete with the pagan Osiris-Dionysus. In a generally acknowledged adaptation of pagan mystical writings, Jesus was created as an answer to the pagan alternatives. They continue to explain that this was not fraud, as the early Gnostic Christians all had an understanding that this was merely a mystical figure, intended to show the way of an enlightened person. They even pose some evidence that Saint Paul could have been one of these Gnostic Christians.

Why then does the modern church believe in the historical authenticity of Jesus so strongly? Two streams of Christianity developed during this historical time, namely the Gnostics and Literalists. The Gnostics always understood the mystical nature of Jesus, but the Literalists were increasingly taking a historical view to Jesus literally – hence Literalist. One has to remember that this happened over a period of 312 years, until Constantine I declared the Literalist stream the official church –

essentially the establishment of the Roman Catholic church. Later, under Theodosius I, the Gnostics were branded heretics, prosecuted, and all their knowledge was destroyed.

Essentially Constantine and Theodosius edited history to include only those Christians who held a firm belief in Jesus as a historical entity, disregarding the Gnostic understanding that this was a mythical figure with very profound and meaningful spiritual lessons for all, but mythical and not historical, after all. From this perspective, it is not difficult to see how the modern-day Catholic Church and the Protestants, as an off-shoot of the Catholic Church, would believe in Jesus' historical authenticity. You don't erase 1 700 years of belief and emotional investment in that belief over night! While *The Jesus Mysteries* did not aim, per se, at doing so, it did ask 'the unthinkable question': 'What if Jesus was not real?'

Even though I had by then abandoned the notion of angels; demons; the Devil; Hell; condemnation; the need for baptism; and practically all other fundamental Christian concepts, I still held a firm belief in Jesus. Not so much in Jesus as savior from sin and eternal condemnation, but Jesus as savior from myself – the one person who had lived the perfect life in order for me to have an example of how to live the life that God had intended for me. This book was a shock to my system. A severe shock, to be perfectly frank. By then I had been in a relationship with Jesus for almost 26 years of my life. Jesus was central to my being, and every bit of investigation and questioning I had done in the name of getting to know Jesus better and living more like him. On a more psychological level, it was probably just the most stable internal object that I had.

Many years ago, in my first year at Stellenbosch, I had faced this crisis of not believing in Jesus' death and resurrection, but never quite engaged with it thoroughly. When I came out of that spiritual desert, there was no space to not believe in Jesus, as he was a practical part of my everyday experience once more. I had always had the knowledge that Jesus' authenticity has no proof; nor does his death or resurrection, which is so pivotal to the Christian faith. The conflict – which is essentially is an academic thesis in book form – was raised in me once more. It was placed in front of me with one hypothesis upon another, the balance of probability being that Jesus was not a historical figure. As an engineer with a scientific mind, I have never been able to argue against science, and I understand very well a 'balance of probability.' It has always been my approach to science that made me challenge God by saying that God cannot be intimidated by science, as he had created the laws upon which science operates. So, if science proves that the world was not made in seven days, or that Jericho had no walls when the Israelites arrived, my belief stood strong that it could not intimidate God. If God cannot rise above such proof at the hands of his own tools (scientific laws), then he is not worthy of being my god or anybody else's, for that matter. My viewpoint has always been that God will rise above this, and that his greatness will shine through as such proof. However, with this book, I was faced with evidence that strongly suggested that Jesus as a historical figure could not be proven for sure. Not only could it not be proven, there was substantial evidence that Jesus was indeed a mythological figure created for particular purposes, the reasons of which had become lost through time with the abolition of Gnosticism.

Not only did this question my faith in Jesus, but, combined with my newly acquired knowledge of how the universe functions through quantum mechanics, it placed a serious burden on my own concept of God. Many years earlier, I found a beautiful concept for God in the later chapters of

The Road Less Traveled (1978), by M Scott Peck. He postulates that from years of therapy and working with the subconscious mind, he is left with little alternative but to conclude that God is in each of us, residing in the subconscious. My own deduction and extrapolation of this notion come close to Yung's notion of a 'collective consciousness.' For many years, I was able to live this understanding of God (The Father), and of Jesus as God-incarnate – as an ultimate example of God's love and how to live an enlightened life – and the Holy Spirit as their agent in us. If Jesus was not real, could my God concept continue to remain the same? I once asked my therapist an unorthodox question regarding her views of God. I understood how unfair this question was in terms of therapist-patient boundaries, but she answered me with a similar concept to mine. As much as I understand now that this was totally subjective and artificial, it gave me the confirmation that I required. God was still what he/she had been made out to be, but Jesus I could no longer believe in.

I had little alternative but to kill or destroy the internal object of Jesus in my psyche. The resemblance for me was similar to finding out after not having contact with a loved one for 26 years that he or she had died shortly after your last contact. In my case it was stronger. Not only did I have to face the loss of Jesus in my life, but more so, I had to face the fact that Jesus had never really existed in my life.

I mourned Jesus' 'death' in my life for weeks, if not months. Every time I thought of it, my heart ached as if I had lost a loved one. I went through the typical stages that one goes through when losing a loved one: anger, denial and acceptance. This took at least three months. I had shared all of this new-found knowledge with Melanie, and she was unperturbed – to her Jesus was real, whether he was historically accurate or not. I've always said that her faith was based on what she felt, and not on what she knew, and so knowing that historically Jesus did not exist changed little of what she felt toward Jesus (this changed over time, so that today she does not acknowledge Jesus' existence either, but will be quick to tell you that it doesn't matter to her). For me, I had to find new definition to my own faith and religion. I no longer believed in Jesus, yet I still believed in God. In terms of my position that Jesus' mission was never to die for our sins, but to show us how to live, the mythical Jesus fulfilled that role adequately. At the same time, my God stillpoint as described during *Manna & Mercy* was still that of an unmoving love for humanity. Under this banner, I could still call myself a Christian and did so for quite some time to come. I understand today that the final step of admitting to myself that I was no longer a Christian was just too big a step, too quickly, and that I was suppressing the question in my head: 'If Christians are people that follow Jesus Christ, then what am I?'

Slowly as time passed, I was able to integrate the question into my psyche, and after a couple of months, I had the courage to admit to myself that I wasn't a Christian any more. This was a surreal feeling and I suspect, paradoxically, a similar feeling to someone who had had a radical conversion. Yet, with this admission, I had changed my identity dramatically. My identity was built around Christianity. Every identity that I had ever adopted pivoted around Christianity. I grew up in a Christian house, with devoted Christians as parents; my cultural identity is one where often the definition of an Afrikaner is linked to being a Christian,[57] and for 28 years of my life I had called myself a Christian. Removing Christianity from my identity left me in a position of having to re-define who I am. This wasn't too dramatic, although it took time for me to get used to the idea of not being a Christian, and even longer to publically admit to this with some degree of comfort. Today I am very comfortable with my history as a Christian, and I understand the contribution it has made to my life, while at the same time I am comfortable with my new identity as a non-Christian.

Many people expect me to carry bitterness, or some level of resentment towards the church and Christianity, and I am often asked what horrible experience I had to make me turn away from the religion. Clearly, this is not the case, and if anything, I have great respect for those for whom it works, and for those who find meaning in the religion for reasons of their own. I am not more outspoken now against those who abuse the principles of Christianity for their own gain; nor am I less critical of fundamentalist Christians.

The question really became: If I don't support the Christian faith or any other religion any longer, what do I believe?

Chapter 10 *Redefining God*

I have an uncle who, at a very early stage in his life, concluded that based on the evidence before him and his scientific inclination, there cannot be a God. My uncle is a retired mathematician, but in his day was one of the world's leading thinkers in the field of systematic analysis.

Of course, this was a major upset in my family, as they considered him 'lost' as an atheist. I grew up with the knowledge that my uncle was 'lost' and we should pray for him. So, it is with immense sensitivity that I have walked my journey, particularly since I have accepted not being a Christian. As I write, my parents and siblings are not aware of this official stance, and while they might suspect it, the severity of the declaration has not been brought before them. Yet, there are so many differences between my story and that of my uncle that I find it important to elaborate on what I do believe today. For a start, I am not an atheist. Atheists by definition don't believe there is a God. Agnostics, on the other hand, claim that there is not sufficient knowledge or evidence for a decision either way, and by implication don't believe either that there is a God or there is not a God. I am neither of these.

It is exactly my quest for God that has made me walk the path I have walked thus far. It is my insistence that what is presented to me by Christians as God cannot be enough; nor does it satisfy my own personal experience and exploration. It is this insistence, over nearly two decades, that has finally brought me to a place where I can no longer be a Christian. Does that mean that I do not believe in God? Does it make me agnostic or atheistic? I believe one first has to dwell on the definition of God before those definitions become valid. For example, if someone defines God as a spiritual being with a personality, emotions and temperament, then God does not exist in my mind. If, however, you define God as the collective sub-conscious of all human beings (and other species), then maybe God does exist. I think the convention when defining individual religious stances is the former definition, and according to that definition, I am a 'nontheist.' A nontheist stands in opposition to a theist, whose specific sense conceives God to be personal and active in the governance and organization of the world and the universe. I clearly do not believe in a personal being that is actively involved in my life and has bearing on my destiny. I do believe, however, that life is not what it seems; that is, there are dimensions, be they spiritual or physical, which we as humans cannot perceive because our senses are too limited as a species, and the universe we occupy is by definition a four-dimensional universe. In these dimensions, there are laws that govern our world and worlds of higher dimensions. In this sense, spiritual dimensions really are just physical dimensions to which we do not have access.

A lot has been written about 'the law of attraction', made popular by the book and short film *The Secret* (Byrne, 2006). The law suggests that you will attract what you put your attention to, whether it is negative or positive. Without judging whether I subscribe to this law as it is presented in all metaphysical literature, it is perhaps sufficient to point out that the double-slit experiment described in chapter 8 above suggests that matter will change its manifestation, based on the observation or the observer's involvement. At the same time, quantum mechanics has established that matter really isn't matter at all, and that all matter is merely very high-frequency vibrations of electrons in super-position, which collapse to one position, based on the level of observation. So, it is conceivable that another physical law, that of resonance, may be at play in our day-to-day lives. Our thoughts and emotions are also merely vibrations, and can be monitored as brain waves and resonance with similar frequencies. Therefore, in my mind, it is quite likely that our thoughts can resonate with other vibrational aspects of the universe, thus influencing the 'matter' of the physical universe. Whether there is hard scientific evidence for this notion, I do not know. What I do know is that some things in life need an explanation. Some people reach for the mystical, and describe all observable yet unexplainable events as acts of God, or angels, demons and other mystical figures. Unlike many atheists and agnostics who choose to deny the unexplained, I, for one, believe that there are real explanations – and we have discovered the roots of many of these, but have yet to find empirical proof, while others we still have no clue about.

I have also started to see the parallels between religion and the scientific world. Rather, I believe I better understand why religious people cling to their religion, based on real experiences; however, I would have different explanations of the mystical from religious people.

Providence and Destiny

Probably one of strongest elements of evidence (albeit not empirical) that religious people put forward for the existence of God are the feelings of destiny and providence. Personally, I have often uttered appreciation for God's plan for my life. I have often felt that God has intervened in my life, and that his plan for my life was too big for me to make certain mistakes. In fact, I often experienced his guiding hand in my life. This was particularly true of the times when I walked away from a bright future with Sasol, against all comprehension, to study theology, and when I decided to move to Johannesburg, and my decision to go to my final interview the day I was job-hunting, which led to my employment with Malcolm at The Marketing Shop. All of these were signposts to me of God's providence and plan for my life, which ultimately translates to my destiny. On a micro-scale, there are numerous examples of how I believed God was guiding me towards his purpose for my life. I was never fatalistic about this, and always maintained that God had certain key junctions that he wished me to arrive at, but the journey between these junctions was entirely up to my free will. Moreover, I held a firm belief throughout my Christian life that God does not act as puppeteer, and even allows sufficient free will for us to choose not to arrive at his desired junctions. As a God-seeking Christian, I had therefore always been grateful when I could 'hear' God's voice, and sense his intervention directing me toward his desired route for my life. This is the experience of many Christians, and many pray for this guidance daily. How then, do I view this today as a nontheist?

In the absence of empirical evidence, what I believe in is as mystical as the beliefs of the theist or Christian who believes in a personified God who guides his children through the wilderness that we call life. I do, however, believe that there is some difference. Quantum physics is increasingly bridging the gap between the physical and metaphysical, and while hard-core evidence is still lacking, there is sufficient evidence in my mind to lead to certain theories and hypothetical conclusions. First, in order to appreciate my experiences, and those of many other Christian, as acts of God or providence, you have to subscribe to time as a linear dimension. At this junction, let us investigate the concept of time a little more deeply.

Just for a moment, view time not as the fourth dimension, but as the third, that is, in the place of height as accepted third dimension (where length and width are the first two). Consider then that length and width form a plane, which we can call the horizontal. Say you make this plane a platform that is height-adjustable in the vertical. If you then place a ruler perpendicular to this plane, and call it time (or height as it is normally called), you can allow the two-dimensional plane to move through the third dimension by adjusting the height of this plane. If you then restrict movement through this third dimension to only being upward (or forward), and only in certain fixed increments, you are restricting the observers on the two-dimensional plane in terms of movement. They can't move down (back) in the third dimension, as movement is only upwards (or forwards). They cannot move upwards faster than the fixed rate; nor can they go upwards a few steps and then come down again. For someone standing in the third dimension (say the lift operator), it would be the most natural thing in the world to see obstacles higher up on the vertical plane and to see the whole vertical axis at once, that is, not as incremental and restricted. For those restricted to the two-dimensional plane, it would be miraculous for someone in the third dimension to have such a complete view of the third dimension (height), while they can only freely move around in the two dimensions (length and width), while moving incrementally and with restrictions in the third dimension.

In reality, this analogy is not far from human beings' experience of time. We are restricted not to a two-dimensional world, but a three-dimensional world. We have complete freedom in these three dimensions and can move forwards and backwards in these dimensions at will, without any restrictions. We are, however, restricted to the fourth dimension, that is, time as we can only move in incremental steps, and only in one direction. Let us go back to our analogy. Let's say those on the two-dimensional plane are not elevated (or liberated) to move freely in the third dimension. The fourth dimension in terms of movement would still bind them.

If you read books by Stephen Hawking (*A Briefer History of Time,* 2005) and others, it soon becomes clear that these higher dimensions are very real, and that while we experience a four-dimensional universe (length, width, height and time), there are numerous dimensions which do not always unfold in the physical universe, but nonetheless exist. Hawking essentially elaborates on Einstein's relativity theory by explaining that gravity around a black hole in space is so immense that for a person who has passed a certain event-horizon, time will continue into eternity at an incremental rate. But, for someone observing this person from beyond the event-horizon, this eternal life would unfold over the period of one second or less. Time becomes completely relative. The ability to look at the fourth dimension also becomes completely relative. In the movie *What the Bleep Do We Know?* there is a beautiful illustration of the beings in a higher dimension of this mystical nature. They illustrate that for someone looking from the top of a maze, it is very easy to direct the actions of those inside the maze, as the latter cannot see the third dimension, while seeing the whole maze at once allows for providence-like guidance to those bound by the dimension. You may ask, who is this guiding force then?

I believe that the universe is far more complex than just four or 12 dimensions, and that what we – who are bound to four dimensions – experience as miraculous is really a normal flow of resonating energy. As we place our intention on certain outcomes, the energy in ALL the dimensions of the universe resonates to yield a totally synchronistic collapse of the wave function toward the result. This result is so incomprehensible to those bound to four dimensions (that is, human beings) that it is experienced as an act of God. This experience is very real for those who experience this mysterious synchronicity in the universe, which is often referred to as coincidence. For me, this is no longer mystical. I have arrived at a point of understanding where I can no longer view this as a personal intervention by a God with a personality, but rather as merely the laws of the universe working together to yield a result that is as empirical as what we can prove in the four-dimensional world, for example the fall of an apple from a tree due to gravity.

Can you appreciate how one electron in our universe can be a wave in super-position with an infinite amount of possible positions throughout the universe (here on Earth, Mars, Orion, etc), collapsing according to the influence of an observer? Then an infinite amount of electrons with the same properties create an unthinkable amount of possibilities. The continuous collapse of these electrons to form our observable universe – bound to only four dimensions – causes this phenomenon that meta-physicists call synchronicity – the universe in synchrony with the thoughts and intentions of you as the observer and the 'all-consciousness' that is observing. This is what religious people like to call providence and destiny, while atheists and agnostics refer to it as coincidence. I also believed it to be providence, but with the evidence before me, I can no longer see the act of an individual God in this process. Rather, I see how my individual role as a conscious being in the universe is able to shape my own reality – whether I am doing it consciously or subconsciously.

Prayer

Let me state categorically that I have always believed in the power of prayer, and still do. My reasons for believing in its power may have shifted somewhat, but I have a very strong respect for people who pray, and the influence that it has on the world. Most cultures, either in a religious or in a personal context, have discovered the power of quietening the mind. Eckhart Tolle's explanation of the mind as almost separate from who I am suggests that the mind clutters the being's perceptiveness of 'what is' other than the four dimensions that our senses can perceive. By quietening the mind, one is able to perceive something greater than the mind. Religious people experience this higher entity as God, while people who meditate experience it as the higher self. Irrespective of the term that is used to describe this perception, it seems to be a temporary liberation from the confines of the dimensional world that we occupy. A study on the 'Maharishi effect', published in 1999 in the *Journal for Social Indicators Research*, suggests that there is a correlation between the gathering of a group of 4 000 participants in the transcendental meditation (TM) and TM-Sidhi programmes in the District of Columbia, and a reduction in violent crime in that city (Hagelin, Orme-Johnson, Cavanaugh, & Alexander, 47, pp 153–201). This correlation is probably the only and closest empirical proof of a connection between a metaphysical act in mediation that translates into some measurable changes in the physical world. Religious people over millennia have numerous examples of prayers that have been answered, which begs the question of whether in time humanity will find a means to measure the results of prayer more frequently and more directly than is currently the case.

I believe that prayer is the process where the intention of the observer is more clearly focused. In the case of the Maharishi experiment, the intention of 4 000 participants was very clearly directed at the reduction of crime in Washington DC.[58] When individuals pray, there is far more focused intention, without the clutter of the mind, on what the conscious being desires, than when this desiring is left to the mind only. Scientists also tell us that the mind cannot distinguish between thoughts and reality, so what the mind thinks or desires will also have a strong importance in the process of focusing intention. It is just that the mind is fickle, and that its desires are often primitive and therefore shift frequently. The conscious being, which is I, has a more consistent intention and therefore a greater focus. In terms of collapsing the wave function(s), I imagine that this focus translates to greater synchronicity, and therefore a greater manifestation of what is intended or prayed for.

Even Christian literature suggests that meditation is an important part of spiritual growth. It is often said that during prayer, you talk to God, and during meditation God talks to you. In both cases, the success of the activity depends on how much you are able to quieten your mind from the persistent stream of daily thought. The absence of this thought seems to be where creation happens. In fact, Deepak Chopra goes so far as to say that creation happens in the gaps between thought. This reminds me of what Stuart Hamerhoff says, namely that on a quantum level we have forty conscious experiences every second, which are strung together like the frames of a movie to give us a reality that our senses can experience. If this is true, then prayer is the process during which we become more aware of the moments between thoughts, which heightens our consciousness, and therefore aligns our intention more strongly, resulting in the collapse of the wave function in a more synchronous way, giving us a stronger perception of the fulfillment of prayer. This fulfillment of prayer is what religious people over the centuries have attributed to God, while I merely see energy in the form of vibrational waves obeying the rules of natural law, yielding – which one can expect when natural law is obeyed. That this all happens in spheres and dimensions that science cannot yet measure fully leaves a big opening for mysticism to occupy its place in our current reality. Let's not forget the cause of disease was attributed to sin and demons not too long ago, until science developed the means to measure the existence of viruses and bacteria. In the same way, what we today accept as quantifiable and scientific was very much mystical as recent as two centuries ago. I believe that in less than a century, the human creative process will have stronger substance in the realm of scientific evidence, and a lot of the mysticism of prayer and the answering of prayers will disappear with that.

A Relationship with the Living God

This was probably one of the last things that kept me believing in God and a relationship with God and/or Jesus. Even after I accepted that Jesus was not a historical figure, my relationship with God was strong enough to let me confess to believing in God and my relationship with him.

I think the most respect that I can allot to this topic is to try to refer to the human capacity to integrate inconvenient truths. Most people have a tendency to go into denial when offered a new reality that does not gel with their existing worldview. This starts at a very young age in Western civilizations. We believe in Santa Claus and the tooth fairy. Early in our lives, we have to integrate the reality that these are fictional figures, and we then have to absorb this inconvenient truth into our realities. Most people do this with great ease and success. Psychologists talk about internal object and object relations. What they refer to is our ability to create mental pictures of our loved ones in such a way that when these loved ones are out of sight, the relationship with them is maintained by the mental image we have formed of them. Babies do this at a very early age, and the first sign that they are able to keep a mental image (albeit for a very short time) in their minds is when they start playing the game of peek-a-boo. Slowly as we grow up, this ability to keep a mental image of those that we love develops so that at a certain stage the mental image of a loved one is as strong as that of our loved one him- or herself.

For most people in a Western civilization, the notion of an invisible but omnipotent and almighty God is a very strong image that is projected throughout society. For me (and I am no expert in this field) it is not difficult to imagine that we create strong mental images of God from a very young age, particularly if you grow up in a religious household like mine. In addition, it is well documented that children often create imaginary friends, particularly when some level of emotional trauma was experienced at critical times in their lives. I have always said that people who are emotionally damaged, are lonely, or have low self-worth have a greater affinity for religion and the church. The church and all its social aspects seem to fulfill a need that these people have in a way that they don't seem to find elsewhere. It is therefore not difficult for me to understand how internal mental images of God, created in a Christian-oriented society throughout all the developmental stages, would allow people to create very strong internal objects associated with God. One's capacity to integrate an inconvenient truth around this object is very much linked to the level of power and fear one has attached to this internal object. To this extent, the thought of God not existing is completely irreconcilable for someone whose internal object is one of a jealous God who will punish those who do not fear him. The fear of punishment and abandonment will create too strong a defense for the inconvenient truth(s) to penetrate. Thus, this type of person will disregard scientific evidence in lieu of a blind faith in God and that associated with God. In his book *How to Know God*, Deepak Chopra explains how your emotional development will shape your own view of God. He explains that our perception of God is linked to our neurological responses to the world. At the most primitive level, this is a 'fight or flight' response that corresponds very much to the vengeance-filled God of the Old Testament. Following that, are the 'Reactive response', the 'Restful awareness response', the 'Intuitive response', 'Creative Response', 'Visionary response', and finally the 'Sacred response' (Chopra, 2000, p. 44). He postulates that our image of God is very much a function of our own emotional development and conscious awareness. The degree to which we operate from the frontal lobe or cerebral cortex is the degree to which we are able to advance to the 'Sacred response.'[59] Each of these responses is associated with the type of God that we will internalize as objects, as well as the type of world we believe God has created. The table below is a summary of the elements in Chopra's book:

Stage	Description of God	Kind of World God Created
1 Fight or flight	God the Protector	World of bare survival
2 Reactive response	God the Almighty	World of competition and ambition
3 Restful awareness	God of Peace	World of inner solitude, self-sufficiency
4 Intuitive response	God the Redeemer	World of insight, personal growth
5 Creative response	God the Creator	World of art, invention, discovery
6 Visionary response	God of Miracles	World of prophets, sages and seers
7 Sacred response	God of Pure Being – 'I am'	Transcendent world

(Chopra, 2000, pp 175–177)

In my case, my make-up as a child made me a perfect candidate to become a passionate follower of God. Not feeling as loved as I should have, and needing a stable figure in my life, God played the part perfectly. He was the unchanging, ever-loving and caring father, which I did not have or the role my father did not fulfill. As I went through my own development up to my early days as a *tokolok*, this internal object was very powerful, as it provided the stability and love from which I could operate. I believe my own development allowed me to migrate my image of God from being 'God the Almighty' as a child through many of these stages as an adult to arrive at the stage where God is not a solemn entity to me any longer. As my own emotional wellbeing changed owing to a greater understanding and healing of my own emotional scars, my capacity to integrate the possibility that God does not exist increased. Let's face it, this is a very inconvenient truth, which I would previously have defended for a long time, purely because my subconscious would not have allowed me to let go of the powerful internal object that I needed in order to function. Increasingly, I depended on this internal object less and less, because I have replaced my internal objects with more healthy objects through years of therapy, and because my capacity to absorb and integrate this truth grew sufficiently strong enough for me to reach a point where I could abandon the notion of God in my life all together. I therefore have great understanding for anybody who believes in God, and continues to believe in God. I witness the various types of God incarnations, as Deepak describes them, very often around me and have empathy because most of these incarnations were very much part of my own make-up or internal object-definition of God at some stage in my life. Don't get me wrong, I am not suggesting that I have arrived, but merely that I recognize that there has been some level of personal development, and that in terms of that development, I no longer need to have a God object in my life for me to function properly.

My journey is one of seeking God, getting closer to what God is, and the role that God plays in my life. I never thought that during my quest I would arrive at a point where God as an individual would lose all meaning to me, but in the greater scheme of things, my appreciation for what God is, is so much bigger today. I have such appreciation for the complexity of the universe, and will continue to study (albeit at a layman's level) the inner workings of the universe and how all of this functions.

In the meantime, I have found a new formed appreciation for spirituality. Where previously religion and spirituality had always been interwoven for me, now in the absence of religion I find a deep need to be more spiritual. I have found expression for this need by investigating many spiritually related topics. In the absence of religious bondage, I have been free to explore many spiritual concepts foreign to, or abandoned by, Christianity. Melanie and I have explored reincarnations and have both had past-life regressions. We explored the transcendental meditation technique with varying degrees of satisfaction.[60]

I have been able to embrace the notion of me as God, without allowing my ego to elevate itself to that of a deity. I understand that we are all God and that within every fibre of the universe there is sufficient information from which the whole universe can be constructed. I embrace all the notions of astronomy and quantum mechanics regarding the physical world and time being mere illusions, and that there is more to life than our senses can observe. Behind this lies a deep need for greater knowledge and a higher understanding of the world. At the core of it lies the need to be free from what Eckhart Tolle calls the ego; to be enlightened; to be connected to the singular consciousness; or better still, to experience myself as being that singular consciousness together with all living things in the universe. If that singular consciousness is called God, so be it. I am free for the first time in my life to explore as far and as wide as I like, and my growth has been phenomenal. I have by no means arrived at a permanent enlightened stage, but I am growing towards that at an exponential rate. I trust my journey might encourage you to have the courage to question. If you do nothing else, just ask the questions. The nature of God or the universe (call it what you want), is such that the answers will unfold in the most exciting ways imaginable. My journey should be witness to God's tolerance for the questioning mind and that it is honoured with answers. This is a thrilling journey, so come and join me. Life is too short to be held captive by what others believe to be God. Go and explore it for yourself. You will be richly rewarded.

Appendices

Appendix A

The French Huguenots and their influence on Afrikaner culture

The Afrikaner nation did not exist before 1652, when Jan van Riebeeck established a Dutch support base for the route to India in the location of modern-day Cape Town. In 1685 Louis XIV revoked the Edict of Nantes and declared Protestantism illegal in the Edict of Fontainebleau. Prosecuted for their religious beliefs, on 31 December 1687 a band of Huguenots set sail from France to the Dutch East India Company post at the Cape of Good Hope, South Africa. These Huguenots, together with the original Dutch colonists, German immigrants and, to a lesser extent, British influences are the ingredients of the Afrikaner nation that would emerge from this melting pot.

What is significant about this is the profound impact that the Protestant Huguenots had on the formation of the Afrikaner culture. Consider that the Huguenots all had a very firm belief system, hence their willingness to flee their country of birth for the sake of what they believed. This classifies their faith as somewhat fundamentalist. Not in a negative sense per se, but rather as illustration of the lengths that they would go to in order to protect their religion.

This group then became a concentrated group with huge feelings of solidarity around their faith, and formed a vital component of Afrikaner culture. It is therefore not surprising that members of this culture – who by their birth had such a strong influence toward fundamentalist Protestants – would have very strong fundamentalist characteristics to this day.

Appendix B

Isaiah 53

1 Who has believed our message
and to whom has the arm of the LORD been revealed?
2 He grew up before him like a tender shoot,
and like a root out of dry ground.
He had no beauty or majesty to attract us to him,
nothing in his appearance that we should desire him.
3 He was despised and rejected by men,
a man of sorrows, and familiar with suffering.
Like one from whom men hide their faces
he was despised, and we esteemed him not.
4 Surely he took up our infirmities
and carried our sorrows,
yet we considered him stricken by God,
smitten by him, and afflicted.
5 But he was pierced for our transgressions,
he was crushed for our iniquities;
the punishment that brought us peace was upon him,
and by his wounds we are healed.
6 We all, like sheep, have gone astray,
each of us has turned to his own way;
and the LORD has laid on him
the iniquity of us all.
7 He was oppressed and afflicted,

yet he did not open his mouth;
he was led like a lamb to the slaughter,
and as a sheep before her shearers is silent,
so he did not open his mouth.
8 By oppression and judgment he was taken away.
And who can speak of his descendants?
For he was cut off from the land of the living;
for the transgression of my people he was stricken. [b]
9 He was assigned a grave with the wicked,
and with the rich in his death,
though he had done no violence,
nor was any deceit in his mouth.
10 Yet it was the LORD's will to crush him and cause him to suffer,
and though the LORD makes his life a guilt offering,
he will see his offspring and prolong his days,
and the will of the LORD will prosper in his hand.
11 After the suffering of his soul,
he will see the light of life and be satisfied ;
by his knowledge my righteous servant will justify many,
and he will bear their iniquities.
12 Therefore I will give him a portion among the great,
and he will divide the spoils with the strong,
because he poured out his life unto death,
and was numbered with the transgressors.
For he bore the sin of many,
and made intercession for the transgressors.

Isaiah 53, New International Version

Appendix C

The Jewish Exile

Most people read the Bible in a chronological format, that is, Genesis was written first, then Exodus and so forth through the gospels right down to Revelations, which was written last. This is not even remotely true.

First, you have to understand the euphoric bubble that the Israelites lived in before 722 BC. First, they believed that they were the chosen people of the living god, Yahweh. Second, they believed that their god was living inside their temple in the most high sanctuary (the holiest of holies). This created an illusion of being untouchable – I would say much like the USA before 9/11 (no disrespect intended).

Then in 609 BC, (there are fierce debates around this date, so if you are interested, Google the subject and enjoy yourself) the Babylonian king, Nebuchadnezzar, started a process of deporting the Jewish nobility, leaders and intellectuals to Babylon. Bible readers would know the most prominent of stories was that of Daniel's exile to Babylon. Nebuchadnezzar also destroyed the temple, along with it, the most high sanctuary.

This was a very volatile time for the Israelites. At the core of the exile lay the question 'Where is Yahweh?' Yahweh's inability to protect his people lay raw in their consciousness and they questioned to whether the destruction of the temple was a sign that Yahweh was not there. This translated into an identity crisis for the Israelites: If we are not the chosen nation, then who are we? Yahweh may not be our god. Then who is our god? Again, the closest resemblance to a national crisis would be the period directly after 9/11. People were disillusioned, angry, scared, lost ...

It is normally in times like this that great leaders are born – people with a great vision for who they are, who their people are, and what their identity as a nation is. Once more, think of Martin Luther King Jnr as a prime example of a leader who rose during a time of crisis. As these leaders rise, they start to write, make public speeches, and communicate the clear visions that they hold.

The volatile state that the Israelites were in made them very susceptible to Babylonian influence. For one thing, their new Babylonian neighbours claimed that their gods created heaven and earth (see the Epic of Gilgamesh), caused the great flood, etc. These were not the stories that the Israelites had been telling around the campfire at night. To them, this was blasphemous, as they believed Yahweh did all the creating. So literature started to emerge, giving voice to the Jewish version of creation. Jewish leaders started to write to defend Yahweh, but also to give identity to the people. The writings were to remind the Israelites that they were 'Yahweh's People' (story of Exodus), that Yahweh was the living god (story of Moses and the burning bush), Yahweh the provider ('Joseph's provision for the Jews in Egypt'), and so on.

Whether these stories are true or not is not very significant. What is significant is the meaning they had for the Israelites. Their truths were told from generation to generation; this was their identity; and this is what the prophets of the day reminded them of.

Few people know that most of the Old Testament was written during and after the Jewish exile. It is a myth that Moses wrote it himself (Exodus, Numbers and Deuteronomy). Linguistic evidence of these books shows that the language used in the original (salvaged from all the bits and pieces) represents the language used during the exile, and not that of a 1 000 years previously (much like we discern that Shakespeare was not written in modern-day English).

The essence of the exile is this: When any nation is in a crisis, the art starts to express this crisis and attempts to attach meaning to the crisis, while regaining identity where this has been lost. Just look at how many movies and books the USA made about Vietnam, 9/11, and the Gulf wars, as an example. It is what people do to cope, and this has not changed over thousands of years. When reading the Bible, one has to consider the context in which these books were written, as well as the purpose for which they were written (van Niekerk, 2008).

Appendix D

John 17

Jesus Prays for Himself

1 After Jesus said this, he looked towards Heaven and prayed: Father, the time has come. Glorify your
Son, that your Son may glorify you. 2 For you granted him authority over all people that he might give
eternal life to all those you have given him. 3 Now this is eternal life: that they may know you, the
only true God, and Jesus Christ, whom you have sent. 4 I have brought you glory on earth by
completing the work you gave me to do. 5 And now, Father, glorify me in your presence with the
glory I had with you before the world began.

Jesus Prays for His Disciples

6 I have revealed you to those whom you gave me out of the world. They were yours; you gave them
to me and they have obeyed your word. 7 Now they know that everything you have given me comes
from you. 8 For I gave them the words you gave me and they accepted them. They knew with
certainty that I came from you, and they believed that you sent me. 9 I pray for them. I am not
praying for the world, but for those you have given me, for they are yours. 10 All I have is yours, and
all you have is mine. And glory has come to me through them. 11 I will remain in the world no longer,

but they are still in the world, and I am coming to you. Holy Father, protect them by the power of
your name—the name you gave me—so that they may be one as we are one. 12 While I was with
them, I protected them and kept them safe by that name you gave me. None has been lost except the
one doomed to destruction so that Scripture would be fulfilled. 13 I am coming to you now, but I say
these things while I am still in the world, so that they may have the full measure of my joy within
them. 14 I have given them your word and the world has hated them, for they are not of the world
any more than I am of the world. 15 My prayer is not that you take them out of the world but that
you protect them from the evil one. 16 They are not of the world, even as I am not of it. 17
Sanctify[b] them by the truth; your word is truth. 18 As you sent me into the world, I have sent them
into the world. 19 For them I sanctify myself, that they too may be truly sanctified.

Jesus Prays for All Believers

20 My prayer is not for them alone. I pray also for those who will believe in me through their
message, 21 that all of them may be one, Father, just as you are in me and I am in you. May they also
be in us so that the world may believe that you have sent me. 22 I have given them the glory that you
gave me, that they may be one as we are one: 23 I in them and you in me. May they be brought to
complete unity to let the world know that you sent me and have loved them even as you have loved
me. 24 Father, I want those you have given me to be with me where I am, and to see my glory, the
glory you have given me because you loved me before the creation of the world. 25 Righteous Father,
though the world does not know you, I know you, and they know that you have sent me. 26 I have
made you known to them, and will continue to make you known in order that the love you have for
me may be in them and that I myself may be in them.

John 17, New International Version

Notes

1. In appendix A I elaborate briefly on the history of the Afrikaner, particularly the influence of the French Huguenots on the Afrikaner culture.
2. Name given to the original church in every town. Literally meaning the 'Mother Church,' from which all congregations grew. Normally this would be a very old and grand building of great stature in the community
3. *'Dominee'* is Afrikaans for Reverend.
4. A youth gathering for the Dutch Reformed children in primary school. The word means circle of children.
5. Christian-National cultural organization with a militaristic undertone, and very much in the service of the apartheid regime. Much of my indoctrination on the political front happened in the organization. The word *Voortrekker* refers to the early Dutch/Afrikaner pioneers of the 19th century in South Africa.
6. 'Prefect' is the term used to describe members of the student council. At our school all prefects were from the final-year students
7. Nickname of the University of the Free State from University Kollege of the Orange Free State (OVS) – UKOS, which became *Kovsies*.
8. *Afrikanerdom*: Afrikaans word for the Afrikaans-speaking nation
9. *Dorpie*: Afrikaans word describing a small town in rural South Africa
10. *Tokolok*: Afrikaans word used to describe a student studying to become a minister at a seminary
11. Plural of *tokolok*.
12. Bachelor of Arts
13. Ants: the name of the governing body of the Student Church
14. The BA Theology that I was studying was often called a BA Admission or just plain Admission. This merely indicated that it was an introductory degree, to be followed by the BTh, which was the degree that allowed admission into the church and ordainment.
15. The Transkei was one of the independent states created by the apartheid government for Xhosa people and the area where Nelson Mandela was born. It was dissolved after the demise of apartheid.
16. See chapter 10
17. Essentially making these my majors together with Philosophy and Theological Studies
18. Small rural town 50 km from Cape Town and at the foot of the Du Toit's mountain range
19. Nickname of the University of Stellenbosch. I am not sure what the origin of the name is.
20. Afrikaans word for form of disco, mostly a pseudo ballroom-type, folk dancing. The word literally means sock.
21. The name of the group. The name is taken from the title of a children's book and is a play on words, referring to the motion of pedalling.
22. Short for Trap der Jeug
23. At that stage, I still believed in angels, demons, the Devil and Hell. See later chapters.
24. Semi-desert area in central South Africa.
25. Student Church.
26. Interesting surname. We used to call him 'Thunderstorm.'
27. Short for 'South African Action for World Evangelization.'
28. An area covered roughly by the 10–40th latitude and longitude lines on the globe, which includes mostly India, the Middle East and China.
29. www.om.org.
30. This is not my position on Muslims, but that held by the OM presentation team
31. House where many young people live together to lower and share costs. In this case, students younger than 25.
32. After the Apostle Paul, who remained in his profession as tentmaker while evangelizing the heathens.
33. Global Conference on World Evangelization
34. Youth with a Mission: www.ywam.org
35. 'Pray through the window', referring to the 10/40 window.

36. Derogatory nickname for conservative Afrikaans people, used mostly by English-speaking people in Johannesburg.
37. Afrikaans word for farm
38. National Association for Automotive Manufacturers of South Africa
39. Dutch Reformed Church
40. Apostolic Reformed Church
41. If you didn't know this already, I suggest you refer to sources outlining the issue, or read a shortened version in my endnotes
42. Were written, as well as the purpose for which they were written (van Niekerk, 2008).
43. In South Africa, vehicles drive on the left side of the road. On freeways, the rule 'Keep left, Pass right' applies.
44. 'For God so loved the world that he gave his one and only Son, that whoever believes in him shall not perish but have eternal life.' – NIV Bible, John 3:16
45. You might want to read a piece I wrote on reading the Bible correctly, in my blog at http://www.louisvanniekerk.com/Home/Blog/Entries/2008/7/3_Reading_the_Bible_correctly.html
46. This is my conclusion, not Erlander's or Alan's.
47. In terms of object-relations a three-year-old child has not developed sufficiently to integrate fully an abstract concept such as God. Children often refer to God, but the internal meaning is different from what is meant by adults
48. 'Jesus answered, 'I am the way and the truth and the life. No one comes to the Father except through me." NIV Bible, John 4:16.
49. Professor Emeritus, Departments of Anesthesiology and Psychology; Director, Center for Consciousness Studies; University of Arizona, Tucson, Arizona.
50. According to Wikipedia, Ramtha is the entity that Knight says she channels. According to her, Ramtha was a Lemurian warrior who fought the Atlanteans over 35 000 years ago. She says that Ramtha led an army of over 2,5 million across the continents, conquering two thirds of the known world, which was going through cataclysmic geological changes.
51. Google 'double-slit experiment' and go to any of the YouTube links. There are many informative video clips on the subject. Or read about it on Wikipedia. Alternatively read about it at: http://www.consciousness-and-spirituality.com/what-is-quantum-physics.html
52. You can read more about most of these topics at my website on Consciousness and Spirituality (van Niekerk, Consciousness & Spirituality, 2009).
53. Examples from a Deepak Chopra seminar attended in Johannesburg, April 2008. No publication available.
54. http://www.washingtonpost.com/wp-dyn/content/article/2007/04/04/AR2007040401721.html.
55. www.skeptic.com. It should offer more than enough material to raise the converse.
56. It was my aim to publish a letter by Heinz R Pagel with permission, as part of the discussion, but I was unable to reach him to obtain such rights. At the time of printing, his letter was published at http://web.archive.org/web/19990420021943/http:/www.trancenet.org/research/pagels.shtml.
57. From www.voortrekkers.org.za, which is the cultural organization called 'Die Voortrekkers' referred to earlier in the text. The quoted Afrikaans portion from the constitution includes a phrase that says that being an Afrikaner includes having a sense of the Christian-Protestant religion. '*Afrikanervolk se wesenskenmerke wat tot uiting kom in sy volkskarakter, omskryf word volgens algemeen wetenskaplike en historiese beginsels wat vir die Afrikaner insluit die Christelik-Protestantse godsdienssin, algemeen aanvaarde waardes, norme, ideale en strewes asook gemeenskaplike kultuurgeskiedenis en tradisies, draer van die Afrikaanse taal, volgens afkoms en keuse uit die Europese volkskultuur, maar Afro-sentries gerig met 'n gemeenskaplike bodemgebondenheid aan Suidelike Afrika. 'n Persoon behoort tot die Afrikanervolk deur afkoms en vereenselwiging of deur vereenselwiging met die wesenskenmerke van die Afrikanervolk; en deur wedersydse aanvaarding.*' (Voortrekkers, 2008)
58. I understand that the transcendental meditation technique does not involve any contemplation during meditation and some may therefore argue that the meditating group was not focusing their attention on reduction of crime. The focus I refer to was the intention of the gathering and group meditation in the first place.

59. This is my personal interpretation, not Deepak Chopra's.
60. While the TM organization maintains that TM is a science and not a religion, I beg to differ. Having been absorbed into the organization for a short while, and having attended some of the Maharishi Open University (MOU) courses and retreats, the religious undertones are tangible. First, on the day of your training, there is sacrificial burning of incense and an offering of flowers, together with chanting in an Indian language, and it is concluded by kneeling in front of an altar. Looking at the MOU, Maharishi is always placed on some sort of throne surrounded by flowers – this position was maintained at all his official appearances until his death. All TM activities that I attended, including a retreat, were filled with religious symbolism, the least of which is the presence of flowers (and no, they were not always just for decoration). This is subtle, but real. Be that as it may. I found the people in the TM organization resembled those in my church gatherings too much, their 'worship' for Maharishi was too absolute, and the symbolism too religion-like for me to feel at home there.

Bibliography

Alsbury, G (Director) (2003). *Consciousness* [Motion Picture].

Byrne, R (Director) (2006). *The Secret* [Motion Picture].

Carrol, R T (1994-2009). *The Skeptics Dictionary.* Retrieved April 2009, from The Skeptics Dictionary: www.skepdic.com.

Chopra, D (2000). *How to Know God.* London: Rider.

Chopra, D (2004). *The Book of Secrets.* New York: Three Rivers Press.

Chopra, D (2003). *The Essential – Spontaneous Fulfillment of Desire.* New York: Harmony.

Dyer, W W (1997). *ManifestingYour Destiny.* London: Element.

Emoto, M (2001). *The Hidden Messages in Water.* Hilsboro: Beyond Words.

Erlander, D (1992). *Manna & Mercy.* Augsburg Fortress.

Freke, T and Gandy, P (2001). *The Jesus Mysteries.* New York: Three Rivers Press.

Hagelin, J, Orme-Johnson, D, Cavanaugh, K, & Alexander, C (1947). Results of the National Demonstration Project to Reduce Violent Crime and Improve Governmental Effectiveness in Washington DC. *Social Indicators Research* , 153–201.

Hamerhoff, S (nd). *Quantum Consciousness.* Retrieved from Quantum Consciousness, www.quantumconsciousness.org.

Hawking, S (2005). *A Briefer History of Time.* New York: Bantam Dell.

Hendrix, H (1993). *Getting the Love You Want.* London: Simon & Schuster.

Howitt, P (Director). (1998). *Sliding Doors* [Motion Picture].

Newton, M (1994). *Journey of Souls.* Woodbury: Llewellyn.

Swindoll, C R (1990). *The Grace Awakening.* Cape Town: Struik.

Tolle, E (2005). *A New Earth.* London: Penguin Books.

Tolle, E (1999). *The Power of Now.* London: Hodder & Stoughton.

Van Niekerk, L D (2008, June). *Reading the Bible Correctly.* Retrieved May 2009, from Louis van Niekerk's blog. http://www.louisvanniekerk.com/Home/Blog/Entries/2008/7/3_Reading_the_Bible_correctly.html.

Various (nd). Wikipedia. Retrieved from Wikipedia. www.wikipedia.org

Vincente, M (Director). (2004). *What the Bleep Do We Know?* [Motion Picture].

Voortrekkers, (2008, April). *Die Voortrekkers: Grondwet.* Retrieved March 12, 2009, from Die Voortrekkers, http://www.voortrekkers.org.za/grondwet/Grondwet_Junie_2008.doc.

Weingarten, G (2007, April 8). *Pearls Before Breakfast.* Retrieved May 25, 2009, from Washington Post, http://www.washingtonpost.com/wp-dyn/content/article/2007/04/04/AR2007040401721.html

Zander, R and Zander, B (2000). *The Art of Possibility.* Boston: Harvard Business School Press.

Zodhiates, S (1996). *The Hebrew-Greek Key Study Bible.* New International Version. Chattanooga: AMG.

www.ingramcontent.com/pod-product-compliance
Ingram Content Group UK Ltd.
Pitfield, Milton Keynes, MK11 3LW, UK
UKHW041944190726
13854UKWH00004B/1782